# STEAM TO DIESEL

*"That kid with the camera"—14-year-old Jim Fredrickson in 1941, holding a* Tacoma News Tribune *press camera.*

# STEAM TO DIESEL

## *Jim Fredrickson's Railroading Journal*

Jim Fredrickson

WSU PRESS

Washington State University Press
Pullman, Washington

WASHINGTON STATE UNIVERSITY

Washington State University Press
PO Box 645910
Pullman, WA 99164-5910
Phone: 800-354-7360
Fax: 509-335-8568
E-mail: wsupress@wsu.edu
Web site: www.wsu.edu/wsupress


First printing 2001

Printed and bound in the United States of America on pH neutral, acid-free paper. 

*Library of Congress Cataloging-in-Publication Data*

Fredrickson, Jim.
Steam to diesel : Jim Fredrickson's railroading journal / Jim Fredrickson.
p. cm.
ISBN 0-87422-245-1 (alk. paper)—ISBN 0-87422-246-X (pbk. : alk. paper)
1. Railroads—United States—History. I. Title.

TF23 .F74 2001
385'.09795—dc21 2001026887

To my wife, Cereta, daughter Kim, and sons Jim and Tim, and to the memory of my father and mother, Martin and Addie Fredrickson.

*Northern Pacific's* North Coast Limited, *Jamestown, North Dakota, June 1940.*

## *Evolution of a railroad photographer.*

This photo of Northern Pacific Class A-3 Northern-type locomotive 2660 was the first reasonably decent train picture I ever took. We were on a family summer vacation in 1940, driving through Jamestown, North Dakota, when I spied this train at the station. Having developed a fondness for trains from previous trips taken by rail to the Midwest, I prevailed on my father to stop so I could take a picture of the 2660 with my new camera. (I'd recently purchased a Kodak *Vigilant* folding camera with adjustable lens openings and shutter speed up to 1/200 of a second. Little did I realize that someday I'd own a camera with the shutter speed of 1/4000 of a second!)

I had come a long way from my first attempt at locomotive photography in 1936, when I tried using a Kodak box camera to photograph one of the NP's Class A-2 2650 series—without notable success. My next camera was a 19¢ Univex plastic camera that fit in the palm of my hand. Its print size was 1" x 1¼". Although I still have a few of its pictures, I did not photograph any trains with it. My Kodak *Vigilant* camera was definitely an upgrade, and I was excited to use it on this vacation.

As frequently happens, this photo included more than just the intended image of the engine. The engineer, shown "oiling around," was a tall fellow, as measured against the locomotive's 6' 5" drive wheels. Farther down the way, a clerk is seen loading mail into the post office car. Attached to the two-year-old locomotive was the coal/water tender, with a handsome, curved design that greatly impressed this 13-year-old. All of the locomotives I had seen around Tacoma had old-fashioned, boxy-looking tenders.

Because my interest was piqued by the likes of hotshot engine 2660, after returning to Tacoma I rode my bicycle to Seattle in search of the newer engines. I was told at the Seattle Roundhouse that there were no such engines out here. (Later I found out why: they were too big to pass through the 1888 Stampede tunnel which had been constructed when locomotives were much smaller.) This news didn't dampen my interest, however, and I continued to visit Tacoma's Union Station with my camera.

I started working in the circulation department at the Tacoma *News Tribune* and became acquainted with the staff photographer, Howie Clifford. He used an immense 4" x 5" Speed Graphic camera which really impressed me. He was a very friendly fellow and with my camera took a picture of me holding his press camera.

In 1943, as a sophomore at Stadium High School, I was photographer for both the newspaper, the *Stadium World,* and the school annual, *Tahoma*. After school hours, I divided my spare time between the *News Tribune* and Union Station. That same year I had simultaneous job offers from both Dan Walton, sports editor of the paper, and Austin Ackley, chief dispatcher of the Northern Pacific. Each asked me to go to work for them. (World War II had created an immense shortage of civilian workers, so they were willing to hire youths like me.) Though it was a tough decision, I chose the Northern Pacific.

I lugged a camera with me wherever I went on the railroad. I dearly wanted a smaller version of Howie Clifford's Speed Graphic, but couldn't afford it, so I settled for an older, used Graflex. The Graflex had a fast shutter for action photos of trains in motion, but a somewhat "long" lens, which made it difficult to get back far enough to fit all of a locomotive in a photo. My next camera was a Kodak *Tourist* folding camera with a fast shutter and wide-angle lens. In the early 1970s, when my son was stationed in Japan on naval duty, he bought me a Mamiya press-type camera. It proved much more versatile than my Kodak *Tourist*. I wore it out, had a replacement stolen, and now possess a third one. These were of the "medium format," 2¼" x 3¼" film size, which I prefer for black and white enlarging. In recent years, I have used a Minolta 35 mm, which is much more compact for traveling.

I possess the negative of every picture I've taken, amounting to roughly 30,000, and I am still in the process of cataloging them. The job should take me well into the 21st century.

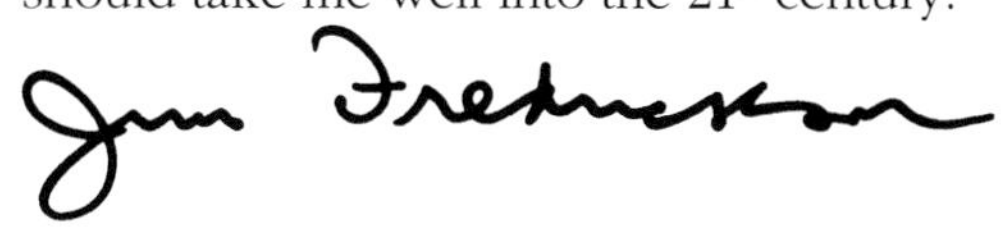

## *NP 5136, "King of the Rails," at Missoula, Montana, August 20, 1949.*

Awesome! Impressive! Majestic!

Words like these are barely adequate to describe the ultimate in steam locomotive technology represented by the 5136, a Class Z-8. I feel most fortunate for two reasons. First, I was able to be there with my camera when this marvel was the "King of the Rails." And secondly, I could do my thing as an "engine picture kid" without getting hassled by anybody. There was no need to get permission from some high-echelon official or to sign a release; no necessity of wearing a hard hat, safety goggles, or steel-toed shoes. Occasionally, if it were convenient, I would stop by a roundhouse office and tell the foreman what I was doing. More often than not, though, I just strolled onto the premises and shot away with my camera.

I remember being challenged only once or twice. One time after the war, when I was at Duluth, Minnesota, the roundhouse foreman came storming out of his office, saying, "No photography!" Fortunately for me, Mr. Ira W. Brewer, whom I knew well, had just been transferred from Tacoma to be the Superintendent of the Lake Superior Division at Duluth. I found a phone, called him, and explained my situation. A few seconds later, the roundhouse foreman's phone rang and, after a brief conversation, he meekly told me to help myself. That happened to be a beautiful morning with perfect lighting. I felt most fortunate to have known a well-placed friend.

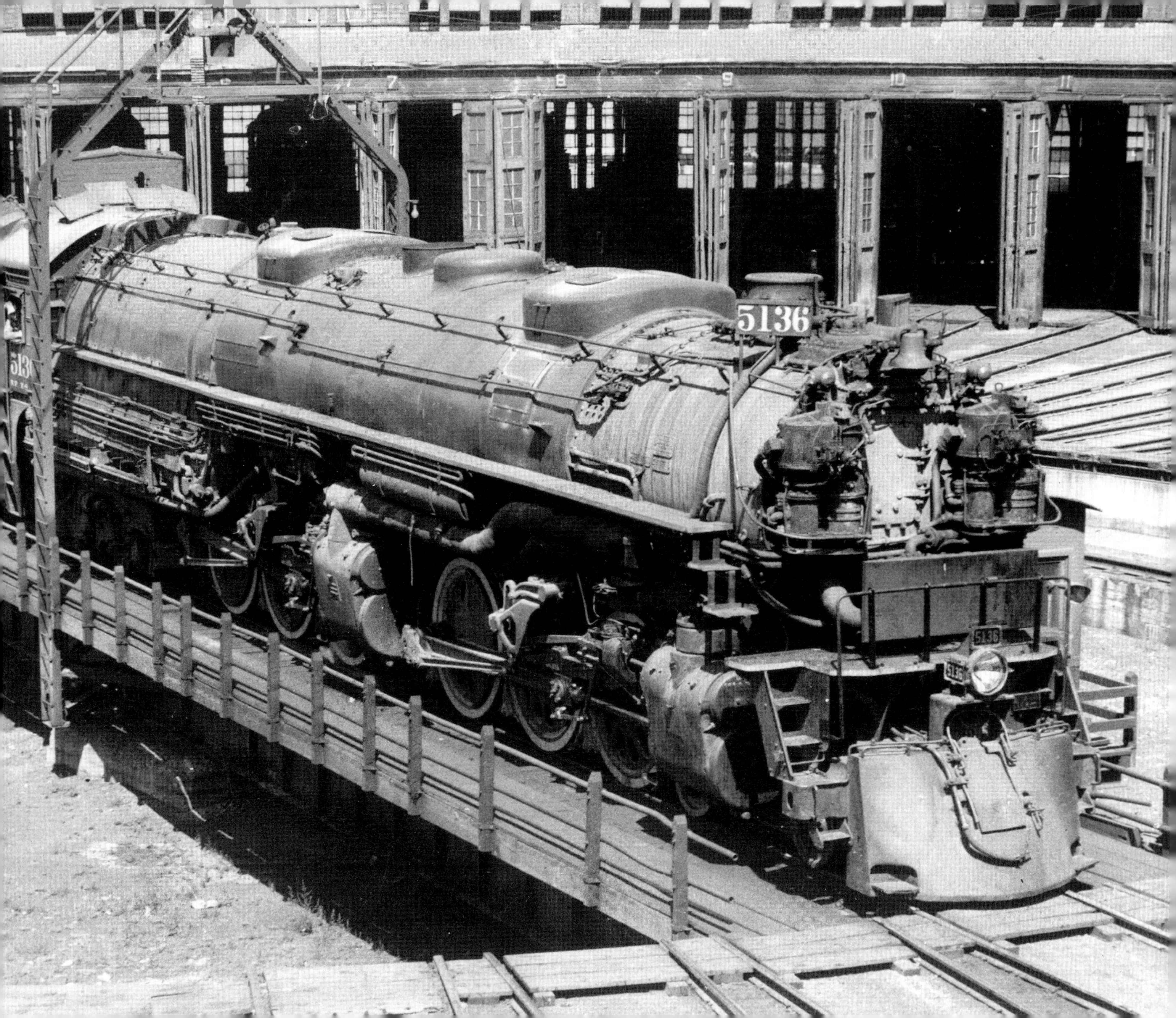
5136

## *Northern Pacific Class F-1 locomotive.*

In 1888, the Baldwin Locomotive Works filled a Northern Pacific order for engines that could climb mountains. Most of NP's previous locomotives had been high wheelers for the minimal grades on the prairies. But now they needed engines suitable for the Rockies and Cascades. These new, low-wheel, "Consolidation" type engines were classified F-1. Designed for heavy-duty work at moderately low speeds, they earned the nickname "Hog." They were still in use when I came to work for the NP in 1943.

The 51 had the distinction of being the engine NP traded to the Polson Logging Company to retrieve the historic locomotive, Minnetonka. When I took this picture in 1948 at Polson's Railroad Camp, 15 miles northwest of Hoquiam, the 51 was awaiting the scrapper's torch.

*The Minnetonka on a Daffodil Parade float, Tacoma, Washington, April 12, 1969.*

The wood-burning Minnetonka was the first locomotive purchased by the Northern Pacific. The Minnetonka, built by Smith and Porter of Pittsburgh in 1870 for $6,700, weighs 12 tons and is 27½ feet long. The engine originally was shipped by rail to Cleveland and then transferred to a Great Lakes steamer for movement to Duluth. From there the Minnetonka traveled to Carlton, Minnesota, where NP track construction had just begun and was put to work on the Carlton to Brainerd segment for about a year before embarking on another long journey. Sent to San Francisco and transported by ship up the coast to Kalama, the engine then went into service building the NP line to Tacoma. When that assignment was finished, the locomotive was shipped by boat up the Columbia to Ainsworth to serve on the main line construction to Spokane.

When the track work was finished, the Minnetonka's NP working career came to an end. In 1886, the engine was sold to B.R. Turner for use in logging operations near Olympia. In 1889, it was acquired by the Port Blakely Mill Company and used for construction of the Puget Sound and Grays Harbor Railroad, a logging line between Kamilche and Montesano. The Minnetonka also was used to transport loggers from their camps to the woods until 1895, when it was sold to the Polson Logging Company of Hoquiam. The locomotive came to be regarded as the queen of the Polson railroad and was lovingly named "Old Betsy." The engine was in regular log hauling service until 1906 and then used for work train service until retired by the Polson Logging Company in 1928.

After rumors reached NP headquarters in St. Paul that the Minnetonka was in the woods somewhere out West, a search was made to locate the historic locomotive. Northern Pacific mechanical officials B.P. Johnson and J.B. Neish made a deal with Polson for an even trade: NP 51—a Class F-1 Baldwin hog—for the Minnetonka.

After a complete overhaul, the Minnetonka began a new and glamorous career in public relations. It became a symbol of NP's extensive contribution to the development of the West and represented the company at a wide variety of exhibitions. It was prominently displayed in Chicago's great railroad pageant in 1933–34, at the New York World's Fair in 1940, and at the Chicago Railroad Fair in 1948–49. NP also sent the engine to a variety of other fairs and celebrations all over the system, including the 1969 Daffodil Festival in Tacoma and the Puyallup valley, where this photo was taken.

The Minnetonka now rests comfortably, still greeting the public, at the Lake Superior Railroad Museum in Duluth, Minnesota.

2611
2611
2611

*NP's "North Coast Limited" with Class A engine 2611, Spokane, Washington, June 1941.*

I now regard a train ride to Spokane in the summer of 1941 as my "mystery trip." I wish I could remember details of this excursion, but most of them have faded into the dark recesses of my mind. I guess that is understandable, since it was sixty years ago.

The previous year I had seen and photographed NP's magnificent Class A-3 and Z-6 locomotives in Montana and North Dakota. I became obsessed with a wish to take more pictures of these mechanical marvels, but was terribly disappointed when I found out that these giants did not venture west of the Cascades.

*Mystery Number 1*—Who told me Spokane would be a good place to find them?

*Mystery Number 2*—Why would my parents let a 14-year-old kid go off by himself on such an adventure? All I can speculate is that because I was an only child, somewhat spoiled, they somehow gave into persistent nagging. I do remember my father telling me to drop the name of his friend, Pierce County Sheriff John C. Bjorklund, in the event of trouble on the trip. At any rate, off I went by myself on Number 411, the connection train to East Auburn, where I boarded Number 2, the *North Coast Limited*, for an all-night ride to Spokane.

*Mystery Number 3*—I took my first trip photo at Lind, of double-header engines 2192 and 2247 taking coal. How did I know I could go that far from my coach without getting left behind? I must have talked to someone on the train crew.

*Mystery Number 4*—Spokane. There are a myriad of questions about my visit there, along with a few vivid recollections. I remember walking up to the head end of the *North Coast Limited* and taking its picture and a "roster" shot of Class A engine 2611. As soon as the train departed, I walked back to the depot and was immediately apprehended by the stationmaster. Though NP's slogan was "Courteous, Friendly," this gentleman showed neither of those attributes. His first question was "Don't you know there is a war on? You can't take pictures around a railroad!" (There *was* war in Europe, but the United States was not yet involved.) Then he ordered me to vacate the railroad in general and his station in particular.

Though the stationmaster had me properly terrified, I was still determined to seek the big engines.

I really don't know how I found out that the NP roundhouse was at Parkwater, about five miles east of the Spokane station, or how I managed to get there. I must have taken a street car or bus, but find it I did. And there they were: Z-6 engines! Unfortunately, because I was still somewhat shaken by the stationmaster's tongue-lashing and was afraid of another confrontation, I hid behind a telephone pole while taking pictures of the engines, and the results were disappointing. I just wasn't close enough for a good photo.

Afterwards, I returned to downtown Spokane and found a location near the depot where I could watch for trains—out of sight of the stationmaster. I photographed a Z-6 engine leaving town on a westbound freight with a Class W-5 helper shoving it on the rear. The sun was in a poor position—but it was an addition for my recently begun train photograph collection.

*Mystery Number 5*—The trip home. I have a faint recollection of staying overnight in a hotel near the station in Pasco. I must have taken evening train Number 3 from Spokane, gotten off at Pasco, and caught Number 5 the next morning. For some unknown reason I didn't take any pictures at Pasco, but did take several from the dutch door in the vestibule of a coach on Number 5.

Photographically, the trip was mostly a bust, but a few of the pictures were passable.

Obviously, the adversity did not discourage me, since, after sixty years, I continue to catch trains in my view finder. Just can't seem to break the habit...

## *Number 408 departing Seattle, Washington, February 16, 1947.*

A photo of a moving steam engine always was enhanced by a large plume of smoke pouring from the stack. The problem was, with a good fireman, just a wisp of smoke usually was visible. Occasionally, photographers tried to get word to engine crews, asking them to make some smoke. But as far as I know, that was not the case in this instance. Because I was puzzled about the reason for the quantity of smoke pouring from this engine, I've asked some enginemen about it. Their best guess is that the fireman on board had gotten "a little behind" and was trying to make up for it. In other words, while sitting at King Street Station waiting for departure, he might have let the steam pressure drop a little too low. He was trying to get it up to the maximum 250 pounds pressure required to maintain Number 408's brisk schedule.

CORRECTED TO OCTOBER 15, 1945

# TIME OF TRAINS

## PORTLAND
## TACOMA - SEATTLE
## VANCOUVER, B. C.

and Branch Lines

—OF—

**NORTHERN PACIFIC**
**UNION PACIFIC**
**GREAT NORTHERN**

Under Pooling Arrangements between Seattle, Wash., and Portland, Ore., Authorized by the Interstate Commerce Commission.

(All trains shown herein operated on Pacific Standard Time).

FOUR TRAINS DAILY EACH WAY
BETWEEN
**PORTLAND-TACOMA-SEATTLE**
IN COMFORTABLE AIR-CONDITIONED COACHES OR CHAIR CARS

Subject to change without notice.

Printed in U.S.A.

TRAVEL IN COMFORT AND SAFETY ON YOUR NEXT TRIP BETWEEN

### Seattle - Tacoma - Portland

SOUTH BOUND

| | King St. Station | King St. Station | Union Station | King St. Station |
|---|---|---|---|---|
| Lv. .SEATTLE | 8.20* | **12.30*** | **4.30*** | **11.30*** |
| Lv. .TACOMA | 9.40* | **1.24*** | **5.45*** | 1.00* |
| Ar. .PORTLAND | **2.20*** | **5.05*** | **9.40*** | 6.45* |

NORTH BOUND

| | Union Station | King St. Station | King St. Station | King St. Station |
|---|---|---|---|---|
| Lv. .PORTLAND | 8.45* | **1.30*** | **4.00*** | **11.30*** |
| Ar. .TACOMA | **1.30*** | **4.48*** | **7.40*** | 5.00* |
| Ar. .SEATTLE | **2,55*** | **5.50*** | **9.00*** | 6.45* |

*—Daily Service.

### For Tickets and Information

VANCOUVER, B. C.
Great Northern, 683 Granville St. Telephone Marine 3627
Northern Pacific, 475 Howe St., Room 207 Stock Exchange Bldg. Telephone Marine 2461
G. N. Station, 1150 Main Street. Telephone Pacific 5511

SEATTLE, WASH.
Great Northern, 1400 Fourth Ave. Telephone SEneca 0400
Northern Pacific, 1401 Fourth Ave. Telephone ELiott 5560
Union Pacific, 1300 Fourth Ave. Telephone ELliott 6933
King Street Station, Third Avenue South and King Street Telephone SEneca 1900, ELliott 5560
Union Station, Fourth Avenue South and Jackson Street Telephone ELliott 6944

TACOMA, WASH.
Great Northern, 116 South Ninth Street Telephone MAin 0113
Northern Pacific, 118 South Ninth Street Telephone BRoadway 1121
Union Pacific, 114 South Ninth Street Telephone BRoadway 2275
Union Station, 1713 Pacific Ave. Telephone MAin 0585

PORTLAND, ORE.
Consoldated Ticket Office, 633 S. W. Morrison Street Corner Broadway—Telephone BRoadway 5631 (Great Northern, Northern Pacific and S. P. & S. Rys.)
Union Pacific Ticket Office, Broadway and Washington Sts., Telephone BRoadway 7771
Union Station, 800 N. Sixth Ave. Telephone BRoadway 3421

### ONE WAY AND ROUND TRIP COACH FARES

Subject to Change.

| BETWEEN | Seattle | | Tacoma | | Portland | |
|---|---|---|---|---|---|---|
| | One Way | Round Trip | One Way | Round Trip | One Way | Round Trip |
| Aberdeen | $2.88 | **$5.20** | $2.04 | **$3.70** | $3.30 | **$5.95** |
| Auburn | .48 | **.90** | .43 | **.80** | 3.60 | **6.50** |
| Bucoda | 1.77 | **3.20** | .94 | **1.70** | 2.28 | **4.15** |
| Castle Rock | 2.66 | **4.80** | 1.82 | **3.30** | 1.38 | **2.50** |
| Centralia | 1.93 | **3.50** | 1.09 | **2.00** | 2.11 | **3.80** |
| Chehalis | 2.01 | **3.65** | 1.18 | **2.15** | 2.04 | **3.70** |
| Fort Lewis | 1.20 | **2.20** | .36 | **.65** | 2.85 | **5.15** |
| Hoquiam | 2.96 | **5.35** | 2.12 | **3.85** | 3.38 | **6.10** |
| Kalama | 3.09 | **5.60** | 2.26 | **4.10** | .94 | **1.70** |
| Kent | .37 | **.70** | .54 | **1.00** | 3.72 | **6.70** |
| Kelso | 2.87 | **5.20** | 2.04 | **3.70** | 1.16 | **2.10** |
| Longview | 2.87 | **5.20** | 2.04 | **3.70** | 1.16 | **2.10** |
| Montesano | 2.63 | **4.75** | 1.79 | **3.25** | 3.06 | **5.55** |
| Napavine | 2.17 | **3.95** | 1.32 | **2.40** | 1.87 | **3.40** |
| Olympia | 1.57 | **2.85** | .74 | **1.35** | 2.70 | **4.90** |
| Portland | 4.03 | **7.30** | 3.19 | **5.75** | ...... | ...... |
| Puyallup | .70 | **1.30** | .20 | **.40** | 3.38 | **6.10** |
| Ridgefield | 3.42 | **6.20** | 2.59 | **4.70** | .62 | **1.15** |
| Seattle | ...... | ...... | .85 | **1.55** | 4.03 | **7.30** |
| Steilacoom | 1.19 | **2.15** | .35 | **.65** | 2.96 | **5.35** |
| Sumner | .65 | **1.20** | .26 | **.50** | 3.44 | **6.20** |
| Tacoma | .85 | **1.55** | ...... | ...... | 3.19 | **5.75** |
| Tenino | 1.68 | **3.05** | .85 | **1.55** | 2.35 | **4.25** |
| Vader | 2.44 | **4.40** | 1.61 | **2.90** | 1.60 | **2.90** |
| Vancouver, Wash. | 3.73 | **6.75** | 2.89 | **5.25** | .30 | **.55** |
| Winlock | 2.30 | **4.15** | 1.46 | **2.65** | 1.73 | **3.15** |
| Woodland | 3.30 | **5.95** | 2.46 | **4.45** | .74 | **1.35** |

| BETWEEN | Seattle | | Everett | | Vancouver, B. C. | |
|---|---|---|---|---|---|---|
| | One Way | Round Trip | One Way | Round Trip | One Way | Round Trip |
| *Anacortes | $2.12 | **$3.75** | $1.24 | **$2.25** | $2.47 | **$4.45** |
| Bellingham | 2.12 | **3.85** | 1.41 | **2.55** | 1.59 | **2.90** |
| Blaine | 2.62 | **4.75** | 1.90 | **3.45** | 1.15 | **2.10** |
| Burlington | 1.61 | **2.93** | .88 | **1.60** | 2.12 | **3.85** |
| Everett | .74 | **1.35** | ...... | ...... | 2.99 | **5.40** |
| Mt. Vernon | 1.52 | **2.75** | .79 | **1.45** | 2.19 | **3.95** |
| New Westminster | 3.35 | **6.05** | 2.64 | **4.80** | .40 | **.75** |
| Seattle | ...... | ...... | .74 | **1.35** | 3.70 | **6.70** |
| Sedro-Woolley | 1.66 | **3.00** | .92 | **1.70** | 2.23 | **4.05** |
| Snohomish | .87 | **1.60** | .17 | **.34** | 3.16 | **5.70** |
| Vancouver, B. C. | 3.70 | **6.70** | 2.99 | **5.40** | ...... | ...... |

All fares in excess of 35 cents subject to Federal Tax.

*Fares quoted to Anacortes apply via Mt. Vernon and Bus. Tickets must be purchased to and from Mt. Vernon.

Stopovers allowed on all tickets within limit.

PROPORTIONATE FARES BETWEEN ALL LOCAL POINTS.

*Portion of passenger service timetable and fare schedule, October 1945.*

## *NP 6510A on the "Mainstreeter" at East Auburn, Washington, platform in September 1962.*

Partially hidden by tall grass and weeds, a concrete platform can still be seen alongside the BNSF Stampede Pass main line at K Street in Auburn. This platform once teamed with activity when it was one of Northern Pacific's busiest but least publicized passenger terminals. The original NP main line went directly to Tacoma, the western terminus, through Enumclaw, Buckley, and Orting. Seattle passengers had to transfer to other trains to reach their destination. But in 1900 the "Palmer Cutoff" was built and then the majority of NP's east-west trains went directly to Seattle through Ravensdale, Covington, and Auburn. However, the railroad did provide Tacoma a connecting service with small two- and three-car shuttle trains known variously as stubs, scoots, vaudeville runs, etc. At first the transfer between the connections and the through trains was made at the downtown Auburn station, but by 1914 facilities had been installed at East Auburn, away from the busy Seattle-Tacoma double-track main line.

Not only were passengers transferred, but there was also a heavy volume of mail and express. The connection train from Tacoma would first stop at the downtown depot where clerks employed there would get on board and go to East Auburn—typically two from NP and three from the Railway Express Agency which had an office at the depot. The baggage cars on the two trains would be spotted opposite each other and an ingenious portable bridge with rollers was placed between the car doors. Veteran clerk Rodger Campbell remembers how heavy this transfer work could be—mail sacks filled with Sears Roebuck catalogs, vats of yeast shipped by express from Sumner (which occasionally fell off the portable bridge and scattered yeast all over the platform), endless empty milk cans (filled going west, empty returning east), and now and then a casket with its occupant going home for burial. That is just a small sampling of the shipments handled by the Railway Express. And then there was mail—up to 700 sacks—transferred from the westbound *Mainstreeter* to its connection.

NP had a substantial passenger business to and from Tacoma. I remember a day during WWII when every seat on Number 4 was taken and benches were set up in a baggage car for the passengers boarding from the connection. NP carman Robert Hoffer lived next to the platform at East Auburn and installed a refreshment stand to serve the many passengers waiting to transfer. This little building with a drop-down front still remains from the glory days of the *North Coast Limited*, *Alaskan* and *Mainstreeter*.

When this photo was taken in 1962 buses and trucks had taken over the Tacoma-East Auburn service. The last train connection was for *North Coast Limited* Number 26 on August 24, 1954.

And now, because Amtrak uses the Stevens Pass line, East Auburn is just a fading memory.

6510A
NORTHERN PACIFIC RAILWAY

*Second 679 crossing Pacific Avenue in Tacoma, Washington, March 10, 1969.*

Just after sunrise, Portland-to-Seattle, hot-shot freight Second 679 crosses Pacific Avenue in Tacoma near the bottom of the South Tacoma hill. It is about to cross the 15th Street Drawbridge on its way to Seattle. Normally, Second 679 would be running on the higher speed Point Defiance Line but was rerouted over the Prairie Line because of the 20-foot-high cars behind the engine. These were cars built specially to carry Boeing airplane wing sections and were too tall for movement via the Point Line. A few years after this photo was taken one of these cars was inadvertently left in a southbound train on the Point Line and collided with the overhead bridge shown on page 29.

*Number 198, Portland to Seattle run, leaving Tacoma, May 1971.*

This photo could be given the title "The Rise and Fall of Passenger Train Glory." Number 198 is the morning Portland to Seattle run then in the second week of operation by Amtrak. Sandwiched between the two former Northern Pacific Vista-Dome cars is a Lewis & Clark Traveler's Rest lounge car. Prior to Amtrak taking over the nation's passenger service on May 1, 1971, these three cars had been assigned to the *North Coast Limited,* which NP proudly called "One of the World's Extra Fine Trains." A few years later they would be replaced by newer Amtrak cars, but fortunately some have been preserved by private owners. The two locomotives were originally owned by the Spokane, Portland and Seattle Railway and pulled the combined *North Coast Limited/Empire Builder* up the Columbia River Gorge to Pasco and Spokane. Lead unit 9758 retains its original paint scheme, but the trailing unit 9756 was repainted with Burlington Northern colors.

The view has undergone a total renovation since this photo was taken. The track department material in the foreground has been moved to a different location. The white building labeled "U.S. Tires" is gone. The parking lot and row of trees have been replaced by the marvelous new Washington State History Museum. The tallest building on the left is the old F.S. Harmon furniture manufacturing building constructed in 1908. It was transformed into the Harmon Pub and Brewery on the Pacific Avenue level, and furnished with 55 apartments above the pub. The 1890s warehouse buildings in the right background are now part of the ever-expanding University of Washington Tacoma Campus. Just to the right, out of the photo, is historic Union Station, now a Federal Court building. Beyond the former Union Station, ground was broken for the new Tacoma Art Museum. Directly behind, across the freight main railroad line, is the 1905 Albers Mill, which will be converted into office and retail space with 24 residential units and parking. Next to it, work is in progress on the Museum of Glass, an international center for contemporary glass art. A 500-foot pedestrian bridge will connect the history and glass museums. I am prouder than ever to be a citizen of Tacoma.

UNION STATION
Coca-Cola
CO-PLY PLYWOOD
NORTHERN PACIFIC
6511
Main Street of the Northwest

## *Number 407 leaving Tacoma Union Station, 1950.*

The fun of photography is being able to look back on good times in the past. This photo gives me a particularly warm feeling. At the bottom of the ramp at track level is my parents' 1940 Plymouth. A few years earlier, it had been purchased new in Nebraska for $650 and we had traveled home in it on old US 30 following the Union Pacific tracks and the old Oregon Trail. My dad, Martin Fredrickson, and my two-year-old son, Jim, are watching train Number 407 depart on its run from Portland to Seattle. Number 407 and its southbound counterpart 408 were the best of the coast line trains and among my favorites.

I spent much of my life at Union Station and the Tacoma Division headquarters. The Dispatcher's Office where I worked is on the right corner of the building on the concourse level. My first acquaintance with Union Station was in 1932 when we went by train to Nebraska.

Many drastic changes have occurred to this scene over the years. All of the industries on the right are gone and the new Washington State History Museum occupies the upper-level parking lot. The station building, beautifully refurbished, is now a Federal Court building. The city of Tacoma owes a huge debt of gratitude to Linda Bowman and Kathryn Van Wagenen, who founded "Save Our Station," a civic group that lived up to its name. Because of their undaunted effort and perseverance, Union Station is now the centerpiece of a dynamic district that is becoming the pride of Tacoma.

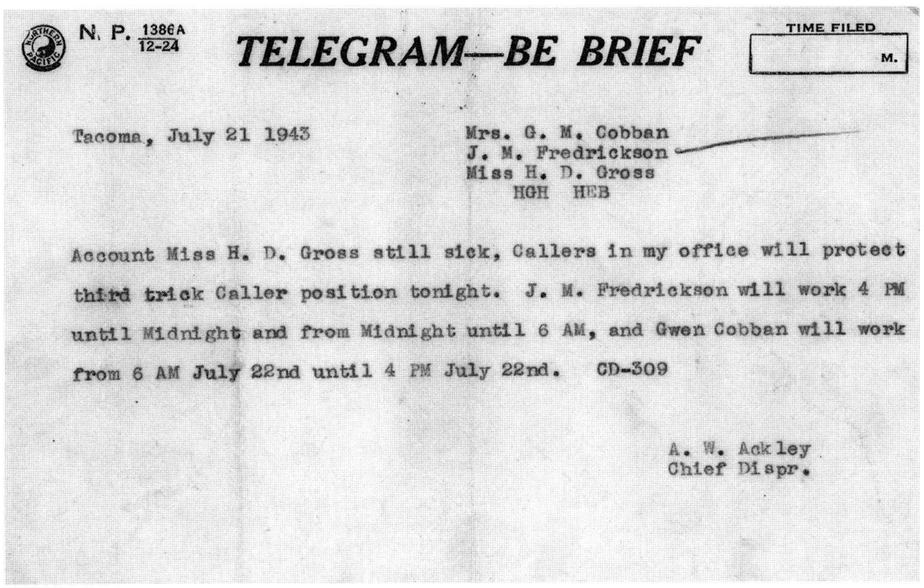

N. P. 1386A 12-24 **TELEGRAM—BE BRIEF** TIME FILED M.

Tacoma, July 21 1943

Mrs. G. M. Cobban
J. M. Fredrickson
Miss H. D. Gross
HGH HEB

Account Miss H. D. Gross still sick, Callers in my office will protect third trick Caller position tonight. J. M. Fredrickson will work 4 PM until Midnight and from Midnight until 6 AM, and Gwen Cobban will work from 6 AM July 22nd until 4 PM July 22nd. CD-309

A. W. Ackley
Chief Dispr.

*Early telegram assigning Fredrickson to two consecutive caller shifts in Tacoma.*

*Tacoma Union Station—evening of the Heart Ball, May 26, 1967.*

*Northern Pacific . . . "Main Street of the Northwest."*

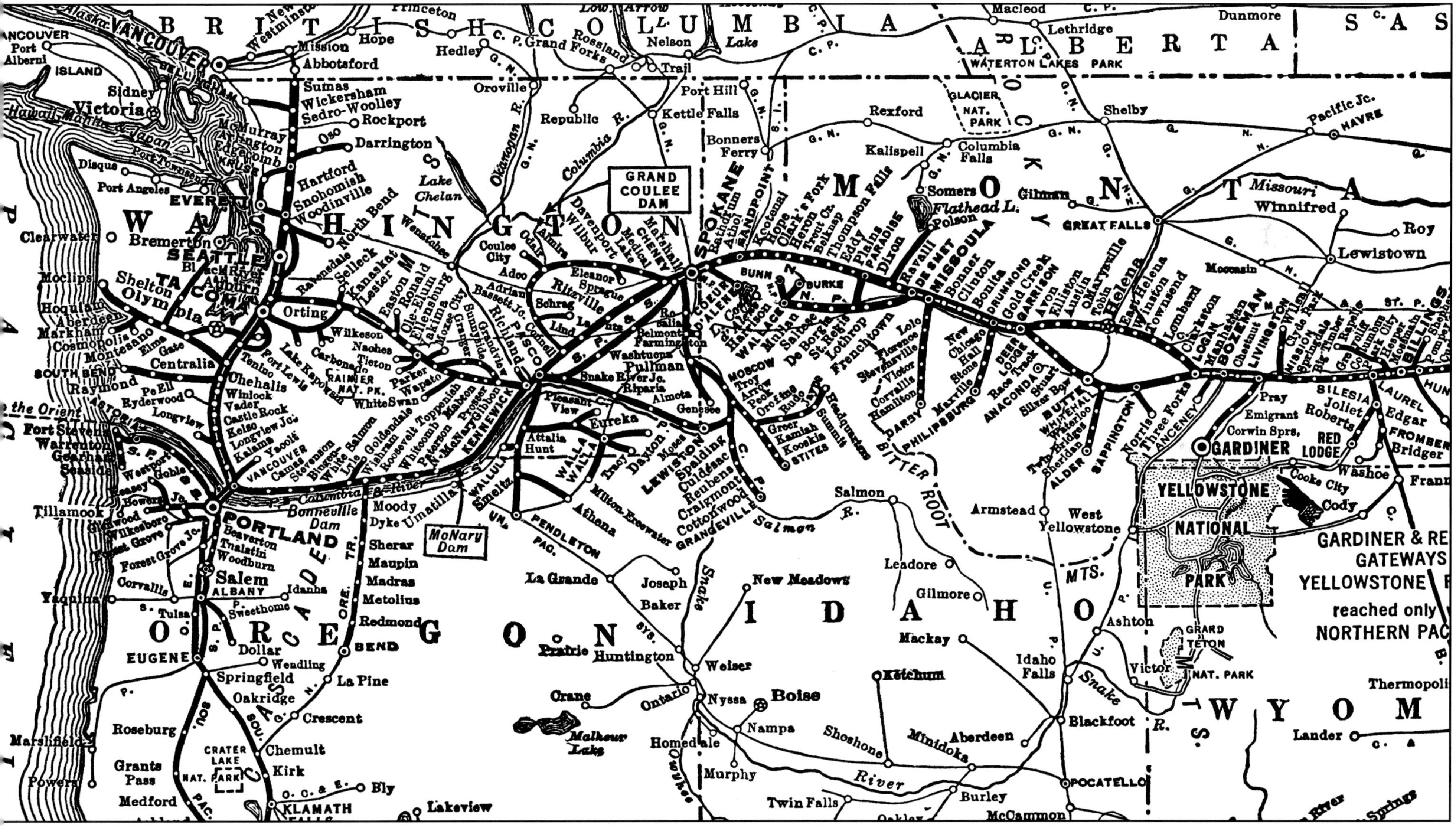

## CB&Q 9946 on Number 199, Tacoma, September 1971.

The Chicago, Burlington and Quincy was a leader in high speed streamliner service with its famous fleet of Zephyr trains. For a number of years, the *Twin Zephyr* held the world's start-to-stop speed record for a regularly scheduled train. Averaging 84 miles per hour, it covered the 55 miles from East Dubuque, Illinois, to Prairie du Chien, Wisconsin, in 39 minutes—including starting and slowing down to a stop. A large fleet of speedy Electro-Motive "E" units was needed for the many *Zephyrs*. A number of them were inherited by Amtrak, which didn't have very many high speed schedules. Some of them ended up in the Northwest—somewhat of a waste of their speed potential—but they were interesting to watch. It just seemed out of place to see a *Zephyr* engine on the Seattle to Portland morning train at Tacoma.

This photo reminds me of two incidents regarding Union Station.

First is the damage caused by the 1965 earthquake, some of which is clearly visible above the arched window. The rotunda inside lost large chunks of ceiling plaster, so the center of the rotunda was walled off until restoration was completed. There also was considerable brick damage to the front of the building.

The second incident deals with the concourse seen projecting out from the main building over the train, with stairs and elevators to the track level. When Interstate 705 into downtown was designed in the 1980s, it was found that the concourse jutted into its path by one foot. Those in charge of the freeway project devised what seemed to be an unhappy solution: build a new Amtrak station on Puyallup Avenue, demolish the concourse, and close Union Station. It was agonizing news at the time, but in the long run everything worked out nicely. Union Station, refurbished as a Federal Court, looks just like new, except for the missing concourse.

9946
BURLINGTON
Burlington Route

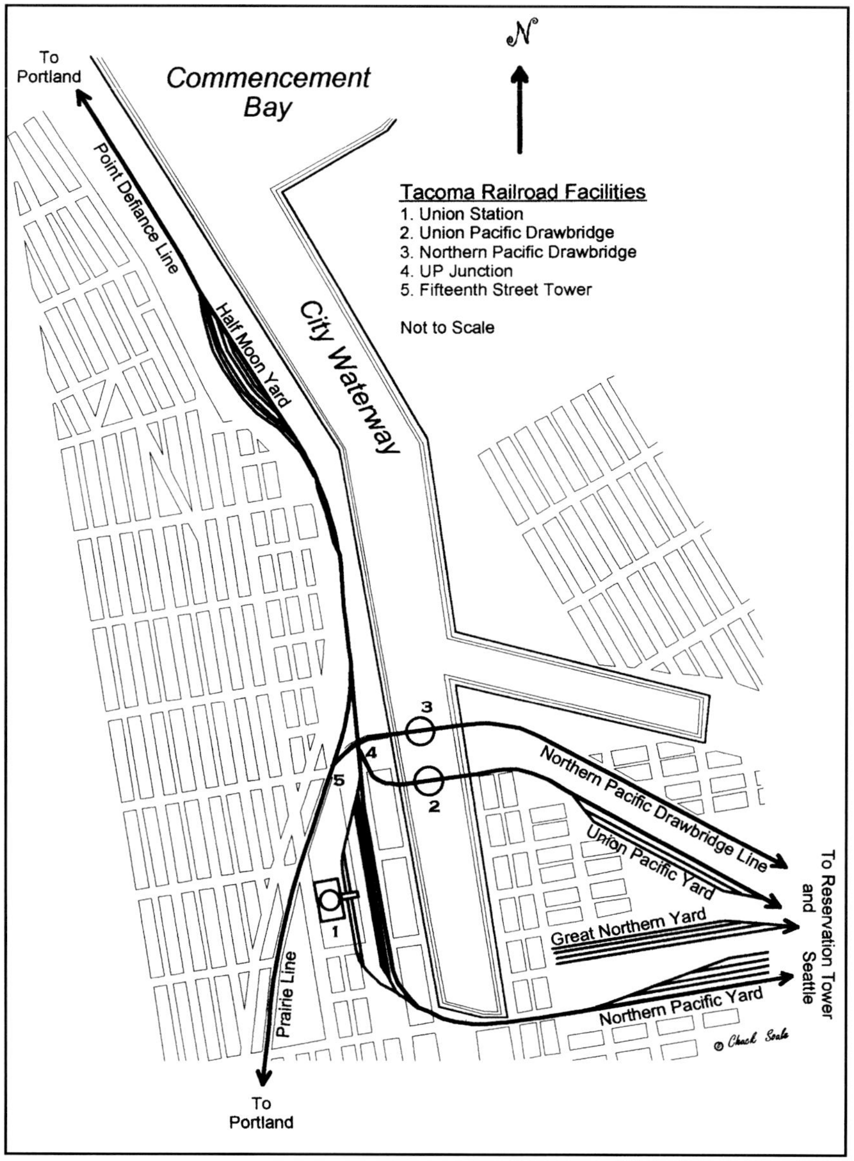


*Tacoma's central railroad facilities.* Chuck Soule

## *Number 408 on the Drawbridge Line in Tacoma, 1967.*

There were two rail routes through Tacoma for many years starting at the Reservation interlocking tower on the Seattle end. The double-track main line closely paralleled Puyallup Avenue, then made a sharp turn at Dock Street to follow the south shore of Commencement Bay, then along Puget Sound to the Nisqually Delta, and on to Portland. The Drawbridge Line left the double track at Reservation, ran along the opposite side of the Head of the Bay Yard, crossed the City Waterway (now known as Thea Foss Waterway) on a drawbridge, and continued on what was known as the Prairie Line up the hill to South Tacoma, Lakeview, Roy, and Yelm, joining the double track again at Tenino Junction. There was also an option at Lakeview of making a right turn onto the American Lake Line through Fort Lewis to enter the double track again at Nisqually.

Nearly all Seattle to Portland trains used the Point Defiance Line, but now and then that line would be out of service. On this day in 1967, a slide near the Narrows Bridge on that line caused a rerouting via the Prairie Line. Train Number 408 (predecessor of Amtrak's *Coast Starlight*) is shown crossing the City Waterway Drawbridge on its way to Union Station to pick up Tacoma passengers. Then it would back out across 15th Street to proceed on the Prairie Line to Lakeview, onto the American Lake Line, and reenter the double-track main line at Nisqually. If there was an obstruction on the double track between Tacoma and Nisqually, southbound trains usually used the American Lake Line and northbound trains ran via the Prairie Line. In effect this made it a double-track operation from Lakeview to Tenino which, combined with the double-track Tacoma to South Tacoma, made South Tacoma to Lakeview the only single-track segment for detoured trains.

Today the drawbridge is gone and the Prairie Line track from Yelm to Tenino has been abandoned and removed.

6706A
NORTHERN PACIFIC
Main Street of the Northwest

## *NP's Mobase Local on the approach to the drawbridge, February 24, 1953.*

Northern Pacific's Mobase Local has just crossed the drawbridge over the City Waterway (now Thea Foss Waterway) and is on what was known as "the approach to the drawbridge." Underneath the approach on the right is the Dock Street Lead and the next two tracks are the double-track Point Defiance main line.

The drawbridge approach created an operating problem. The height of a car in a train on the Point Defiance Line passing underneath was limited to 18' 5" to clear the approach. When the Point Line was built in 1914 this posed no problem, but as car size increased in later years many could not fit beneath the overpass. The solution was to move those cars onto trains running overhead on the Drawbridge/Prairie lines. The tall cars would be cut out of southbound trains at Tacoma Yard and sent to Tenino Junction on the Mobase Local. Northbound trains would set out high cars at Tenino Junction for the Mobase. The northbound Portland-Tacoma Time Freight was assigned to run via the Prairie Line for the express purpose of handling high loads via the Drawbridge. Occasionally, a priority train such as NP Second 679 would be rerouted via the Prairie Line to expedite the movement of a high load.

My good friend, Assistant Chief Dispatcher Don McGregor, was fond of saying, "There's many a slip 'twixt the cup and the lip." The remark comes to mind as I recall a night in 1973 when a 20-foot-high Boeing wing car, similar to the one pictured on page 18, was overlooked on a southbound train. It clobbered the drawbridge approach as it passed underneath it, causing considerable damage to both the bridge and the car. After that episode, Burlington Northern decided that the drawbridge and its approach were no longer of great importance and removed them.

The bridge visible in the background has a clouded future. The historic 11th Street Bridge, recently renamed the Murray Morgan Bridge, has been declared unsafe for future use. The present options are to rebuild it, build a modern bridge at a lower cost, or to simply dismantle it.

The two tall smoke stacks in the picture belonged to the now defunct Consumers' Central Heating Company, which supplied heat to many downtown buildings.

1800
1800
NORTHERN PACIFIC
LOW CLEARANCE

*Two helper engines pushing the Long Hill switch drag, Tacoma, 1953.*

The Northern Pacific constructed the sea-level Point Defiance Line from Tacoma to Tenino in 1914 to avoid the 2.2% mountain grade on the Prairie Line from Tacoma to South Tacoma. Even though the majority of trains used the new line, a fair amount of activity continued on the Prairie Line over the years. Great Northern continued to use it until 1943. Hoquiam passenger trains, troop trains, the Mobase Local switching Prairie Line stations, the Gate Local bound for Olympia with loads of logs that couldn't go through the Nelson Bennett Tunnel, and Portland-Tacoma Time Freight with high and wide loads all made use of the Prairie Line. If the Point Defiance Line was blocked by a wreck or slide, all trains were rerouted to the Prairie Line.

Also using the Prairie Line were the switch jobs for all of the industries from downtown Tacoma to South Tacoma, including the NP shops. First there was the Long Hill crew which went up the hill in midmorning to take care of the Nalley Valley area. There were lots of cars for Nalleys, Sears Roebuck, and others in this locality. This was the case on the morning this photo was taken, when two helper engines were needed to get the train to the top of the grade. Next, in late afternoon, came the Short Hill crew, which switched for the brewery and other industries and warehouses along Commerce Street. Finally, the South Tacoma job took the many cars going to NP's South Tacoma Shops and neighboring customers.

1694
1694
NORTHERN PACIFIC
1780
1780
CENTRAL

RESERVATION
SOUTHERN PACIFIC
6387

## *NP train Number 685 departing Tacoma, October 22, 1967.*

Train 685 originated in Eugene, Oregon, on the once great Southern Pacific Railroad, which later became part of the Union Pacific system. NP and SP had a run-through agreement for NP locomotives going to Eugene and SP engines heading to Seattle; the crews from the respective roads changed in Portland. SP locomotive 6387 was called a "covered wagon," the original design for freight diesels.

Reservation Tower stood at the Seattle end of Tacoma Yard, just beyond where the I-5 highway bridge crosses over the tracks. This view shows a number of relics from a bygone era. Starting at the left, a train order delivery rack can be seen with its inserted forked devices known as "hoops." The looped string in a hoop was held in place by a metal clip at the base of the fork. After train movement instructions (train orders) were dictated by a Tacoma Union Station dispatcher to an operator at Reservation, these written orders were put in the hoop strings and held in place by slip-knots. A passing engineman would put an arm through the fork and snatch his orders from the top string; a trainman in the caboose at the rear would take his orders from the lower string.

Just to the right of center stands a signal mast with two semaphore blades, called a train order signal. The black blade signaled trains on the northbound track; its 45-degree angle informed train personnel that they must secure train orders to proceed, but could do so "on the fly" without stopping. If the black blade had been in a horizontal position, it would have indicated that the train must stop for orders. The other semaphore blade governed traffic on the southbound track; the perpendicular, "clear" position in this photo meant "no orders" for trains on that track.

*Tim Fredrickson at work at Reservation Tower in 1971.*

Inside Reservation Tower were 32 "armstrong" (meaning hand-operated) levers that lined switches, locked them, and gave proceed signals to trains. The switches were connected to levers by a series of rods made out of ordinary iron pipe. This enabled the telegrapher/towerman to line the proper route for passing trains. There were a number of options: through on the double-track main line; to and from the 15th Street Drawbridge Line; in and out of Northern Pacific's Head of the Bay yard; and Union Pacific trains to or from a connection to the Milwaukee Road—either to or from the UP yard or to or from the NP main line. Great Northern trains (which operated over the NP) also used the Drawbridge Line to access their freight yard.

Every operator who worked at Reservation has to remember lever number 7, which lined the distant crossover switch for UP trains coming off the NP. Because I was still a scrawny kid when I worked at Reservation, I didn't have the brute strength required to move the levers without difficulty; it required a certain "swing" for me to pull one all the way.

I enjoyed my job as an operator at Reservation because there was endless activity. During World War II, one 4 P.M. to midnight shift particularly stands out. I had 44 trains come through in 8 hours—almost one every 10 minutes. Lining the routes and getting orders for so many trains was an intense, unforgettable experience. Because the train order delivery rack devices had not yet been installed, I had to stand by the track and hold hoops close enough to the engines for the crews to grab their orders. The interlocking procedure required that I wait for the engines to go by the "home" or entrance signal, then throw the signal lever to stop position, grab an armful of hoops, bolt through the door, race down the steps, and cross to the northbound track just in time to deliver orders to the engine thundering by. The ultimate thrill for me was handling NP hotshot passenger train Number 407, particularly when I had to deliver orders on the fly to both engines when there was a doubleheader on the train.

Now Reservation Tower is gone and a distant dispatcher electrically operates remote control switches. Furthermore, the old written train order system is obsolete and dispatchers send instructions by radio directly to the crews on the trains.

I'm glad I was there when it was fun.

*Canadian Pacific 2387 in Vancouver, British Columbia, June 15, 1953.*

One of the things I like best about living in the Pacific Northwest is the close proximity to Canada in general, and Vancouver in particular. Our first visit to this wonderful, cosmopolitan gem of a city was in June 1953, and we couldn' t have picked a better time. Everywhere we went there were banners celebrating the coronation of Queen Elizabeth II. Her loyal Canadian subjects were brimming over with excitement.

And, the Canadian Pacific roundhouse was only a few blocks from our hotel. I've returned many times since, both on family holidays and business trips during my last job with Burlington Northern. Pictured here is CP passenger locomotive 2387, a 4-6-2 Pacific type.

*British Columbia Electric Ry. Co. 1315 in Vancouver, June 15, 1953.*

This electric streetcar's photo was taken at Jubilee Station during my first trip to Vancouver. The subject of historic streetcars always brings to the forefront of my mind the name Warren W. Wing. He published a beautiful book, *To Seattle by Trolley*, with sharp, clear photos of Seattle streetcars and the city's outlying interurban lines.

Warren cannot remember when he was not a railfan—he is one of us who seemed to be born that way. Raised in West Seattle, he often rode the trolleys, including a memorable ride downtown in 1927 to see the famous aviator, Charles A. Lindbergh. Warren enlisted in the army immediately after Pearl Harbor and was sent to Cook and Bakers School in San Francisco. After graduation, he was assigned to a troop train as mess sergeant. This enabled him to see the United States by rail, although he found it most challenging to acquire food and prepare meals for 250 men aboard a train. After the war, Warren worked for the U.S. Postal Service as a letter carrier. His favorite routes, of course, were those near the rail yards in Seattle.

After retiring in 1973, Warren was able to devote more time to his railroad history interests, and did a wonderful job locating historic photographs. His first book, *A Northwest Rail Pictorial*, included photos by Albert Farrow, as well as some of mine.

## *Esquimalt and Nanaimo train Number 1 at Nanaimo, British Columbia, August 9, 1956.*

The Esquimalt and Nanaimo Railway was purchased by the Canadian Pacific in 1905 and passenger operation was taken over by VIA in 1977. I first rode the E&N *Dayliner* in 1956 with my two sons. A big thrill for the boys on this trip was at Nanaimo when a Canadian "Mountie" came aboard, resplendent in full-dress uniform.

The history of the E&N is as colorful as Vancouver Island's beautiful scenery. It was incorporated in 1884 through the efforts of Robert Dunsmuir, a powerful British Columbia politician and industrialist who had large coal-mining interests on the island. His cohorts were Charles Crocker, Leland Stanford, and Colis P. Huntington, who were driving forces in building the Central Pacific portion of the first transcontinental line in the United States. The Southern Pacific town of Dunsmuir, California, received its name as a result of this friendship.

The E&N had more than its share of construction and operational problems, such as when its first steam locomotive accidentally fell into San Francisco Bay while being loaded on a ship for Victoria. Nevertheless, passenger service began on September 24, 1886, and rose to 100,000 people a year by 1900. Handsome, red passenger cars with polished mahogany interiors and a parlor car with a brass railing observation platform were used on this run until 1955, when replaced by diesel Budd cars.

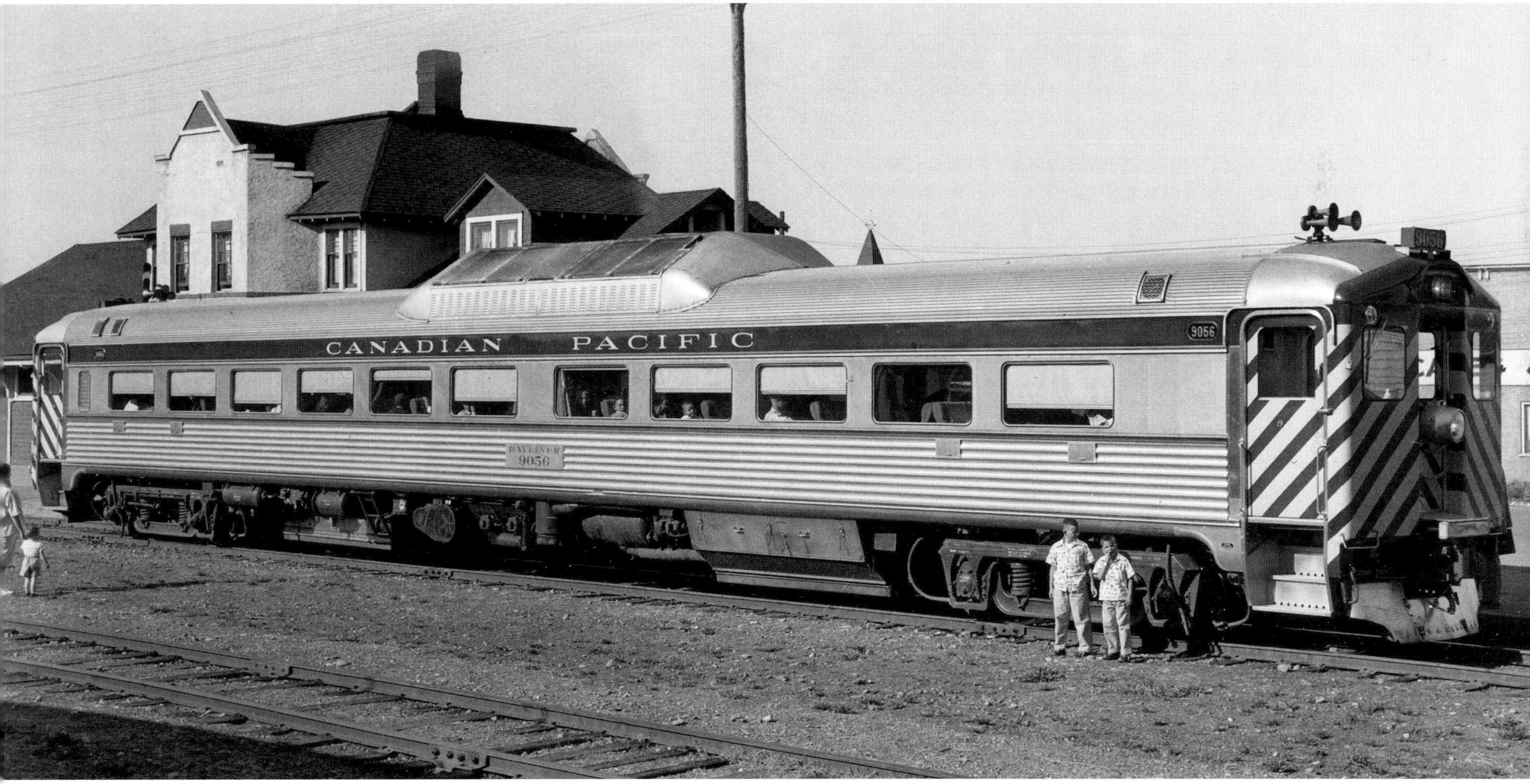
CANADIAN PACIFIC
9056
DAYLINER
9056

## *Class Z-3 Mallet 4025 on the Dorsey Trestle, May 28, 1952.*

My wife, Cereta, was born and raised in St. Maries, Idaho, on the main line of the Chicago, Milwaukee, St. Paul and Pacific Railroad. Over the years, we periodically visited her sister, Gabrielle, and her husband, Joe "Sully" Sullivan, who still lived there. That's where we went for our 1952 vacation—to the beautiful country on the banks of the "Shadowy" St. Joe River. St. Maries was not far from the nearest Northern Pacific line, making photo excursions reasonably easy.

Early one morning, Cereta and I, accompanied by our four-year-old son Jim, set out from St. Maries for Wallace, Idaho, to catch the NP in action. The plan for the day was to follow the daily freight from Wallace to the main line at St. Regis, Montana, from which point the engine would return to Wallace. We arrived at Wallace just in time for the 7:00 A.M. departure. We drove US 10, which followed reasonably close to the railroad most of the way to St. Regis. The sky was clear, and the local had a good engine for photos—a Class Z-3 Mallet 4025. Couldn't get much better than that!

After a quick shot at Mullan, we scurried ahead to the Dorsey Trestle. What a dandy spot for a photo—quite close to the highway. This high, spindly trestle, that looked too frail to support a brute like the 4025, was rebuilt after 1910 when a mammoth forest fire put it out of commission. (The "Big Blowup" of 1910, which burned three million acres, claimed the Dorsey Trestle. Resourceful railroaders and patrons kept traffic moving while repairs were made. Trains would stop on one side of the damaged bridge, where the passengers then would get off, walk to the other side of the canyon, and board another train.)

After shooting the 4025 on the trestle, we drove on to the summit of Lookout Pass.

SOUTHERN

*NP 4025 at Lookout Pass, Montana, May 28, 1952.*

I was just about standing on the Idaho-Montana state line when I took this picture at Lookout Pass. The grade from just east of Mullan to Dorsey is 2.2 percent, "mountain grade," which is the maximum for almost all mainline operations. The grade from Dorsey to the top of Lookout Pass is a monumental 4 percent—difficult, but acceptable on a branch line. It was a challenge for a locomotive, but the effort would cause large clouds of smoke, which was terrific for photos.

Originally, it was intended that the line over the top would be temporary while a lower-level tunnel was constructed to reduce the grade to a standard 2.2 percent. Though discussed for years, the tunnel never was built. *Railroads through the Coeur d'Alenes,* an excellent book by John V. Wood, gives a detailed account of the building of this line and others in the area. It is illustrated with many photos taken and collected by Ronald Nixon.

## "JJ on Little Goliath," May 28, 1952.

Saltese, Montana, is located near the bottom of the Lookout Pass grade. At one time, Saltese had a two-stall roundhouse and turntable for Lookout Pass helper engines.

Here the crew of the 4025 went to the town restaurant for "beans," thereby providing an opportunity for me to take a photo of our four-year-old son on the engine. Cereta kept a log of the pictures taken on the trip; her entry for this one reads, "JJ on Little Goliath." In his very early years, we called him Jim Jim; now everybody calls him Fred. He had a favorite storybook which described the adventures of a brave little engine named Little Goliath. We had told him earlier in the day that we were following his storybook's engine.

The 4025 had served on the Tacoma Division at one time. Her partners, the 4023 and 4024, were old friends of mine from the Tacoma Division, both being road engines from Auburn to Yakima and helper engines at Easton and Lester. These three were my favorite Z-3s because they were the only ones that had both air pumps on the front of the smoke box, giving them an intimidating appearance. (Engine 4021 had a single pump on the front, which looked sort of odd.)

251

## *Milwaukee Number 18, the "Columbian," leaving St. Maries, Idaho, May 27, 1952.*

The *Columbian* was the Milwaukee Road's counterpart to the Northern Pacific's *Alaskan* (later *Mainstreeter*) and the Great Northern's *Western Star*. These three trains had one thing in common—they were scheduled through the gorgeous scenery of northern Idaho and western Montana during daylight hours. Ironically, the more illustrious premier trains of the three roads went through after dark, particularly on short winter days.

Leaving eastward from St. Maries, Idaho, the Milwaukee closely hugged the banks of the "Shadowy" St. Joe River for 45 miles to Avery. Then came a spectacular crossing of the Bitterroot Range.

The *Columbian* was a comfortable train with reclining-seat lounge coaches, diner-lounge car, tourist sleepers, and Pullman Standard sleepers. There was one significant difference between it and the *Olympian Hiawatha*. Between St. Maries and Missoula, the *Columbian* had 2 regular stops and 23 stations where it could be stopped on flag. The *Olympian Hiawatha* had 1 regular stop and no flag stops.

On a memorable ride in the electric locomotive cab of a westbound *Columbian*, I counted 8 bridges and 22 tunnels between the west portal of the Taft Tunnel at Roland, and the town of Avery, a distance of 22 miles.

*Milwaukee Number 263 crossing Benewah Lake Trestle between St. Maries and Plummer, Idaho, May 27, 1952.*

Today, this 2,200-foot long wooden pile trestle adjacent to the south end of Coeur d'Alene Lake is one of the last remaining segments of the old Chicago, Milwaukee, St. Paul and Pacific Railroad west of Terry, Montana, that still is in use—albeit by another railroad.

The Milwaukee Road, as it was known for short, was the last of the northern transcontinental lines to be built. None of the northern transcontinentals have been able to maintain their original identity; the Northern Pacific and Great Northern became components of a new company, the Burlington Northern, in 1970; and ten years later, the bankrupt Milwaukee ceased operating. Much of its track was torn up, but Potlatch Forests, Inc., acquired 64 miles of the main line from Plummer to Avery, Idaho, and a 53-mile branch from St. Maries to Bovill, Idaho.

Potlatch established a new company—the St. Maries River Railroad—with headquarters in the ex-Milwaukee station in St. Maries and commenced operation on May 23, 1980. Potlatch had a large mill at St. Maries and needed rail service for hauling logs in and the finished product out. There are several other customers to keep the railroad going, including the Regulus Mill at St. Maries, garnet operations at Emerald Creek, and Kimberly Clark's pulp log dock at Tyson Creek. The St. Maries River Railroad connects with the Union Pacific at Plummer, and at one time had a direct link to the Burlington Northern at Bovill at the south end of its branch line. (The old Washington, Idaho and Montana line from Bovill to Palouse had become part of the BN, but floods in 1996 severed the connection at Bovill and it has not been reestablished.)

The Avery Logger made its last run in 1984 and the track was removed in 1987. Service continues from St. Maries to Plummer on the main line, and from St. Maries to Clarkia on the branch.

*Milwaukee Number 264 passing along the North Fork of the St. Joe River, Idaho, August 20, 1970.*

It's a 45-mile drive by automobile from St. Maries eastward to Avery, Idaho. The first 23 miles to Calder has long been a paved road, but the last 22 miles to Avery formerly was a rough, rocky, single-lane dirt road, with frequent logging trucks to contend with. That was before the Milwaukee was abandoned. Now the roadway from Calder to Avery has been moved onto the old railroad right-of-way and is paved.

The attractions of Avery as a destination point more than made up for the discomfort of the trip on the old roadway. What a marvelous place to photograph trains! The Milwaukee Road was electrified over the Cascades, as well as across the Bitterroots and Rockies, with a 227-mile gap from Othello, Washington, to Avery, along which steam and later diesel power was used. That meant that almost every train changed or added engines at Avery.

On this bright August day east of Avery, train Number 264 pulled in with three diesels and "Little Joe" electrics E-73 and E-21 were added to the point. It's a 1.7 percent grade to the top of St. Paul Pass, with an elevation gain of 1,678 feet in 22 miles. The track on one side and the road on the other followed the North Fork of the St. Joe River. It's absolutely stunning scenery!

The story of the "Joes" is intriguing. The Soviet Ministry of Railways ordered 20 locomotives from General Electric in 1946, but, by the time they were built in 1948, the "Cold War" had broken out and President Truman put a ban on the sale of strategic materials to Russia. Railroad locomotives were classified as "strategic" and General Motors had to find other customers. The Milwaukee bought 12 of them, 3 were sold to the Chicago, South Shore and South Bend Railroad, and 5 to Brazil. An unknown Milwaukee employee christened them "Little Joes," after dictator Joseph Stalin. E-70 has been donated to the city of Deer Lodge, Montana, and is on display near the courthouse, looking beautiful in fresh orange and black paint.

Noel Holley's *The Milwaukee Electrics* tells the fascinating story of the Joes in detail.

*Kim Fredrickson (with her dog, Fritz) and cousin Erin Sullivan at St. Maries, Idaho, July 1968.*

My daughter Kim was born relatively late in Northern Pacific history—after steam engines had been retired from the railroad, and just ten years before the NP was combined with the Burlington Northern. Consequently, she was more rarely featured in train-related photos than her older brothers. In my collection, photographs of Kim tend to emphasize other types of adventures that she brought into our lives, including attending President Jimmy Carter's inauguration, working for the Equal Rights Amendment (ERA) in Oklahoma, and visiting the home of Hollywood stars Bobby Van and Elaine Joyce. I have fond memories of these special times shared with Kim.

*NP 305-306, the "Doodlebug," November 25, 1952.*

NP Passenger Department Circular 48-1952 contained eight pages outlining all of the changes that were to take place in passenger service effective November 16, 1952.

There would be a dramatic speedup of the *North Coast Limited,* and the *Mainstreeter* was to be established. In fact, there were revisions across the entire system; last on the list was reviving Train 305-306 between Spokane, Washington, and Paradise, Montana, which the circular said would be provided by a Gas Electric Motor Car. That was half right. Two "doodlebugs" (also known as "galloping gooses") were assigned to this run—gas electric B-18 and diesel electric B-23. The *North Coast Limited* made no stops between Spokane and Paradise, and the *Mainstreeter* stopped only at Sandpoint and Thompson Falls.

Number 305 and 306 would fill in the gaps, which were many: Otis Orchards, Hauser, Rathdrum, Athol, Granite, Cocolalla, Kootenai, Hope, Clark's Fork, Heron, Noxon, Tuscor, Trout Creek, Belknap, Eddy, and Plains would all have the benefits of NP passenger, and mail and express service—such as it was. There was a wide gap between the comfort of a modern, quiet, streamlined coach on the *North Coast Limited* and the noisy, rough-riding, galloping goose, which truly lived up to its nickname.

We were in Idaho for Thanksgiving when the changes took place and I seized the opportunity to take my one and only doodlebug ride. I rode all the way from Spokane to Paradise and back. It was a dark, overcast day and I didn't take enough pictures. Wish I could do it again.

NORTHERN PACIFIC
NORTHERN PACIFIC
5005
5005

*NP 5005, Class Z-5 "Yellowstone," at the coal dock in Livingston, Montana, May 23, 1952.*

The diesel-electric locomotives of today are marvelous machines with incredible power, utilizing sophisticated computers. Unfortunately, they don't have the personality and variety that steam engines did. Most diesel-electrics are made by just two manufacturers, General Electric and General Motors, which sell the same models to all railroads. Steam locomotives, on the other hand, were custom built to meet the needs of individual roads. And, of course, a steam engine could put on a spectacular show with smoke and steam belching from its stack, accompanied by a thunderous roar.

The Northern Pacific needed special locomotives to solve an operating problem on the Yellowstone Division between Mandan, North Dakota, and Glendive, Montana. With an undulating, roller coaster-like grade extending for 216 miles, it was necessary to divide trains in two or doublehead them for movement across the western badlands. NP asked the American Locomotive Company (Alco) to design an engine that had enough power to make train splitting unnecessary.

The result was the world's largest steam locomotive—actually two locomotives under one boiler—called a simple articulated. This mammoth engine was 125 feet long and weighed 1,118,000 pounds. It was 16 feet, 4 inches high from top of rail to top of stack, and the tender carried 21,200 gallons of water and 27 tons of coal. It rolled out of Alco's Schenectady, New York, plant in December 1929, numbered 5000, Class Z-5. It was named the Yellowstone type in honor of the division for which it was built.

The NP and Alco jumped at the chance for publicity, and photos of the 5000 appeared in newspapers throughout the country, often in Sunday rotogravure sections. Alco staged a banquet for 12 people in the firebox, which had a grate area of 182 square feet. The firebox was equal in size to a room 22 feet long, 9 feet wide, and 7 feet high. After a year of testing, NP asked the locomotive builders for bids on 11 additional Z-5s. This time the Baldwin Company was the winner, underbidding Alco by $7,000 per locomotive.

Although periodic modifications were needed, the Yellowstones did the job they were built to do by eliminating the Mandan to Glendive bottleneck. They held the "World's Largest" crown for a dozen years, until losing it to the Union Pacific's Big Boys in the early 1940s. The final blow to their lofty status came in 1944 with the arrival of NP's first Electro-Motive FT road diesels. Two Z-5s remained for a time on the Yellowstone Division, but the rest were transferred to the Rocky Mountain Division, primarily for helper service at Livingston and Helena, until the scrapping process began in the 1950s. The last engine to go was 5001, dismantled at Brainerd, Minnesota, June 6, 1957.

It's such a shame that none were preserved! What a monument to the steam age it would have been if a 5000 could have been placed in a Mandan or Glendive park.

*Three diesels (two F-7s, one F-3) at Glendive, Montana, April 26, 1950.*

I first stopped over in Glendive, Montana, in 1946 because of a quirk in train schedules. I was on my way to Chicago aboard Number 4, the *Alaskan,* which arrived at Glendive at 1:15 A.M. and departed at 8:40 A.M.—a 7 hour and 25 minute stop. It had something to do with a North Dakota state regulation that required railroads to provide day service across the state. Employee passes weren't good on the *North Coast Limited,* which went by us at 5:50 A.M. That was fine with me. It gave me a chance to see a gigantic Yellowstone Class Z-5 engine. As soon as dawn broke I was out with my camera and, luckily, was able to capture the 5009 ready to leave town on a westbound freight. The deep-throated roar that came forth when the engineer pulled back on the throttle made the long layover absolutely worthwhile.

I made a number of visits to Glendive over the years and always found something that made me glad I was there—like the day in 1950 when these three diesels, quite by accident, were lined up in perfect position for a portrait. The 6007 and 6011 were almost new F-7s and, strangely, the 6000 was an F-3 originally numbered 6011.

I only regret that I was not able to have been in Glendive before the war to chase the Yellowstones by auto to Beaver Hill, Sully Springs, and Medora. Fortunately, Warren McGee was there and I take consolation when I view his classic photographs of the Yellowstones in all their glory.

# Here's how to make pictures from the Vista-Dome

GOOD pictures can be made with most any type of camera in black and white or in color, by following a few simple precautions:

1. Do not lean arms on the window frame or any part of the car body. Cameras should be cushioned in the hands, elbows close to body, to prevent vibration from being transmitted to the camera, resulting in blurred image in the picture. Avoid shooting directly into the sun.

2. If you are using a simple camera with fixed shutter speed, aim at distant scenes ahead or to the rear rather than to the side to avoid blurred foreground. Cameras with shutter and lens adjustments should be set for as high speed as conditions will permit to reduce motion to the minimum.

3. Hold camera as close to the window as possible without touching it. This helps eliminate reflections which might be encountered. Movies are sometimes improved by running camera at 24 or even 36 frames per second instead of the normal 16. This produces a semi-slow motion effect when projected to improve scene definition.

## EXPOSURE

1. If you are using an exposure meter with color film, your meter reading will tell you how to set your lens and shutter. If exposure chart or table is used, increase lens opening 1½ stops.

2. For black and white film use meter reading. If exposure chart is used, increase lens opening 1 stop.

## FILTERS

The glass in the Vista-Dome is tinted to eliminate sun-glare and absorb heat. It also reduces light to some extent. From a practical sense, good pictures can be obtained in either color or black and white without the use of filters. But when color film is used a noticeable greenish cast will result, especially if compared to pictures made outside the train. If you have one of the popular Skylight filters, it will help to slip it over the lens of your camera.

For those who wish to go into the more technical aspects of color photography, the use of Kodak Filter CC30-R or CC20-R is recommended to compensate for the tinted glass in the Vista-Domes. With the use of either filter, lens opening should be increased 2/3 stop if meter is used, or 2 stops if exposure chart is used.

On the back page are listed some of the highlights of Northern Pacific's scenic route, which offers many interesting and inspiring subjects for photographing. Good shooting to you!

G. W. RODINE, Passenger Traffic Manager,
St. Paul 1, Minn.

*A* North Coast Limited *Vista Dome promotional brochure: "Shooting tips for camera fans" (1956).*

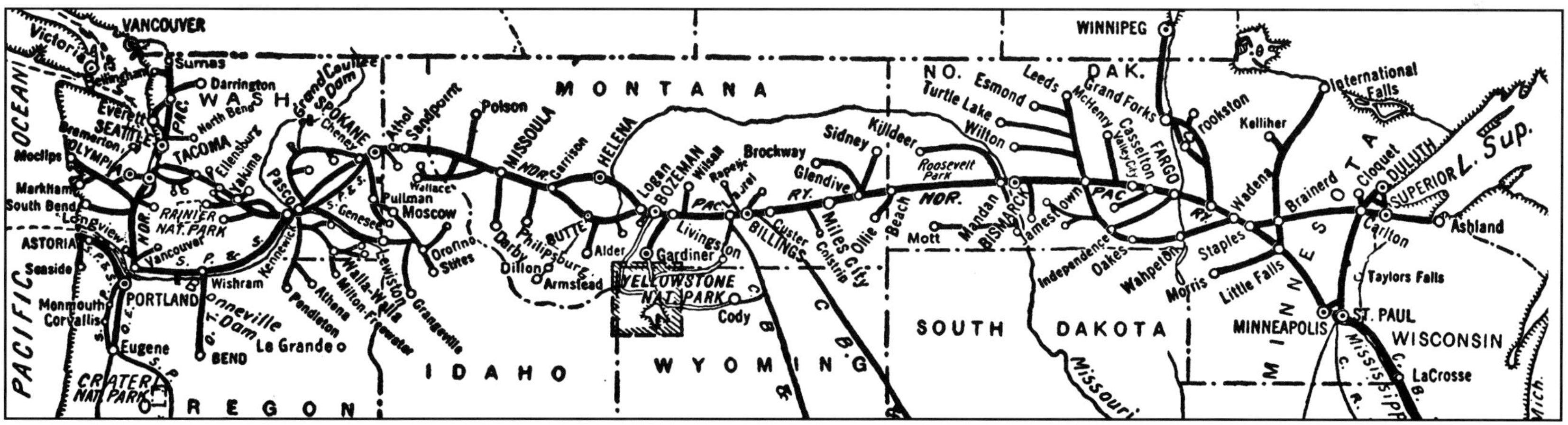


*Northern Pacific Railway passenger time table map, 1967.*

*Number 651 from Laurel to Butte, Montana, three miles from the summit of Homestake Pass, September 2, 1972.*

Two slogans used on the cover of Northern Pacific passenger train guide books were "2000 Miles of Scenic Beauty" and "Scenic Route Across America." However promotional they might sound, these words were absolutely true; there was an incredible variety of scenery for the transcontinental traveler.

Starting from the west and heading east, on the *North Coast Limited* I always enjoyed riding in the dome car and listening to the "oohs" and "aahs" of people from the flatlands as they marveled at the many crossings of the Green River and the climb over Stampede Pass with the beautiful waterfall coming down over the east portal of the two-mile tunnel. The Yakima River Canyon from Ellensburg to Yakima was a just-before-dinner treat; big, brown hills loomed up and suddenly the train would veer around them. Yakima to Spokane lacked raging rivers and towering peaks, but one night in the dome car we viewed a meteor shower that was spectacular.

The ride along Lake Pend Oreille and the Clark Fork River from Sandpoint, Idaho, to Paradise, Montana, was stunningly beautiful. On sunny, calm days we could see the mountains twice—in their reality and in the mirrored reflection in the lake. The next sight heading east was the rugged Coriacan Defile and the Marent Trestle, the highest on the Northern Pacific.

After Missoula, Montana, came the Hell Gate Canyon, followed by a split in routes at Garrison. *North Coast Limited* passengers who traveled via Butte witnessed one of the most awe-inspiring segments of the railroad—the Butte Mountain. This high country made it obvious how the Rocky Mountains got their name.

Passengers on the *Mainstreeter*—and before that the *Alaskan*—traveled via Helena and Mullan Pass. Although not as rugged as the Butte Mountain route, it involved a steep climb with many hairpin curves. Afterwards, the train climbed Bozeman Pass and then descended into Livingston with another breathtaking view—the Absaroka Mountains.

After Livingston, Montana, the mountain show was over, but the trains followed the Yellowstone River and passengers soon were treated to the rugged beauty of the western North Dakota badlands. East of the badlands, North Dakota was mostly flat farmland, but a spectacular sunset often ended a perfect day.

The photo shows a sample of Northern Pacific scenery. The locomotive units were once NP but now display Burlington Northern numbers. The consist is BN 826-831-832-9828. Before March 3, 1970, they were NP 7006D-7008C-7009A-6707A. The telltale warns anyone on top of the cars that the train will soon be going through short tunnel number 3.

826
832
9828

1355
FRITZ'S CORNER
PIPES CANDIES TOBACCO
Coca-Cola
Fritz's Corner
CIGAR STORE
Warm Reception
COLD BEER
FRITZ'S
CORNER
BEER
PARCELS CHECKED
PARKING
NORTHERN PACIFIC

*Northern Pacific local freight switching in Coeur d'Alene, Idaho, June 10, 1955.*

The Northern Pacific's many branch lines were all served by local freight trains. The crews on these runs were well acquainted with their customers and would drop off cars at industrial sites for loading and pick them up when ready to go. In Coeur d'Alene, a train is chuffing along Third Street on its way back from a sawmill on Coeur d'Alene Lake and soon will be departing for Spokane. The boxcars are loaded with lumber.

Today this scene is totally transformed. The tracks have been removed from the city center and Fritz's Corner with its "warm reception" and "cold beer" long ago was replaced by a bank. The Greyhound bus terminal has been moved elsewhere and the Resort Plaza shopping complex now occupies this block.

Coeur d'Alene is at the end of what was known as the Fort Sherman Branch of the NP. General William Tecumseh Sherman had investigated this area in 1877 (the year following Custer's Little Big Horn fight), looking for prospective sites for forts to keep the peace between Indians and white settlers in the Interior Northwest. One of his selections was a beautiful spot on the north shore of Coeur d'Alene Lake at the head of its outlet, the Spokane River. Sherman's recommendation later was approved and 999 acres were set aside for a military post called Fort Coeur d'Alene and the town grew up around it. Sherman visited again in 1883; and, when he retired in 1887, the fort was renamed in his honor. Fort Sherman closed in 1900 and now a city park and North Idaho College occupy part of its grounds.

*NP "Mainstreeter" Number 2 at Thompson Falls, Montana, July 1968.*

Train and engine crews held the general opinion that dispatchers could enhance their train-movement skills by getting out "on the road" and taking a first-hand look at the territory. Consequently, most engineers welcomed a dispatcher aboard without an engine pass or written permission, even if the dispatcher was off his home division.

Such was the case on a sunny summer day when I was aboard the *Mainstreeter* en route east. I walked up to the engine in Spokane, introduced myself as a Tacoma dispatcher, and engineer Bob Alexander said, "Welcome aboard." That was the beginning of a lasting friendship, as we discovered we had much in common: we both were photographers, historians, and collectors.

The *Mainstreeter* had one edge over the *North Coast Limited*. It was scheduled over an absolutely gorgeous, scenic segment of the Northern Pacific in daylight hours, while its otherwise superior partner came through during the night. The most incredible scenery began with the mile-long bridge over Lake Pend Oreille at Sandpoint, Idaho, followed by many miles along the lake and the Clark Fork River. In my early trips, the single most spectacular spot was rugged Cabinet Gorge, which has since been obliterated by the Cabinet Dam.

At Thompson Falls, the Paradise-Trout Creek Local and its GP-9 engine was waiting in the clear for us, contributing to the photo opportunity.

## *Engineer Bob Alexander.*

Engineer Bob Alexander's family homesteaded near Spokane, Washington Territory, in the 1880s. His father, Elmer Alexander, spent some time prospecting in the Colville-Chewelah area and, together with some others he had befriended, staked a claim to what later became the Old Dominion Mine. Elmer stayed behind to watch over their find while the others went to Spokane to file the claim. While on his watch, another group came upon the scene and tried to jump the claim. (One of that bunch carried a famous name: Wyatt Earp.) But Elmer refused to back down, and, because others in the valley rushed to his support, he succeeded in holding the claim.

The Alexanders continued living on the Spokane-area homestead and by the time Bob was born in 1911, a second house had been built. The east end of today's BNSF Yardley yard occupies a part of this property.

Bob went to work for the Northern Pacific as a grease monkey as soon as he graduated from high school in 1929. He and his wife Irene were married in 1932 after she had graduated, and they had four children. Though he was unemployed a number of times during the Depression, once for nine months, they survived the hard times until he became a fireman on August 24, 1936.

Engineers soon found that he had a real knack for giving them a full head of steam and he was rated one of the best firemen on the Idaho Division. His reputation was confirmed in 1942 when he was selected to be the fireman from Paradise, Montana, to Spokane on President Franklin D. Roosevelt's secret inspection train to the Northwest. Bob was promoted to engineer on July 1, 1943.

In later years, with his seniority, Bob could have whatever run he wanted. He chose the *Mainstreeter* over the *North Coast Limited* because it was a day job with great scenery and a mid-day layover in Paradise, where he could go hiking and catch up on letter writing. I always enjoyed receiving his interesting, information-filled letters. He retired in 1975 after forty-six years of service.

*Swede's Place in Garrison, Montana, June 6, 1955.*

This is a scene from the *real* "Wild West," located alongside the track at Garrison, Montana, just east of the depot. It was a favorite watering hole of local "rails," particularly the gandy dancers.

Swede took care of his railroad patrons. For their own good, he would collect their checks on payday and dole out money for living expenses until the next payday. He'd see to it that not too much went for entertainment.

There's not much left at Garrison now. The depot's been torn down, Swede's is gone, and passing motorists zipping by on Interstate 90 hardly notice this once-active little community.

*"Mainstreeter" with the Washington Club car at Garrison, June 6, 1955.*

Northern Pacific provided, in effect, a limousine service by rail for Tacoma passengers with shuttle connection trains between East Auburn and Tacoma. The Rocky Mountain Division had two counterparts to the East Auburn operation: at Garrison and Logan, Montana, for the benefit of Butte and Helena passengers. The Northern Pacific mainline divided at these two towns, with a northerly line through Helena and a southerly route through Butte. The *North Coast Limited* ran via Butte, with either a train or bus connection to Helena from Logan and Garrison; the *Alaskan,* and its successor the *Mainstreeter,* ran via Helena, with connecting service to Butte.

This service provided some interesting options when the schedules allowed. Once, when coming west on the *Alaskan,* I changed to the Butte connection at Logan, continued on through Butte to Garrison, and reboarded the *Alaskan* there.

This photo was taken a little over two years after the *Mainstreeter* was established, but before its new Holiday Lounge cars had been received. In the meantime, heavyweight Pullmans with eight sections and a lounge were borrowed for this train. The Washington Club in the photo was owned by the Atlantic Coast Line. Other early *Mainstreeter* lounges were from two New York Central companies, the Michigan Central and the Cleveland, Cincinnati, Chicago and Saint Louis (better known as the Big Four.) The lounges included the Garrison Club, Knickerbocker Club, Ridgewood Country Club, Yondotega Club, and Youngstown Country Club.

By the mid-1950s, buses were exclusively handling the Butte/Helena connecting service—about the same time buses replaced trains between Tacoma and East Auburn.

Peter Thompson, a friend of mine in Nottingham, England, and I share one love in addition to the NP. It's a 1950s British movie called the *Titfield Thunderbolt,* starring Stanley Holloway. Peter sent me a videotape of the movie and a book about its production, both of which I treasure. The storyline has to do with a successful revolt by local citizens after learning that the operators of a unique little train intended to replace it with a bus. The uprising was bankrolled by Mr. Holloway's character, who pledged his support on the condition that there would always be a bar car on the train. The movie strikes a chord in me, since the events in it took place at about the same time that the NP was replacing the East Auburn, Garrison, and Logan trains with buses.

### *First 603 at Bozeman, Montana, June 7, 1955.*

Over my 70-plus years I have visited every state in the Union except Alaska, eight of the ten Canadian provinces, Mexico, and recently made it "across the pond" to England and Scotland. Though I have had many memorable experiences, I never enjoyed a day any more than I did on June 7, 1955, in Bozeman, Montana. We had traveled from Tacoma to Livingston, Montana, to visit the Warren McGees. I accompanied Warren to his Northern Pacific assignment as conductor on the Bozeman switch. It was a glorious day, with perfect weather and unrelenting activity on the railroad. Of course, the highlight was seeing and photographing both the eastbound and westbound *North Coast Limited.*

Another impressive train sighting was hot-shot First 603 with 71 loads, 2 empties, 3554 tons, and Conductor Benson and Engineer McGuire. At this particular spot there weren't any mountains or rivers to embellish the scene, but the sky made up for it with a fine assortment of cloud formations. When there were no trains passing by on the main line, I enjoyed watching Warren McGee and his crew at work. Warren railroaded like he photographed—with perfection. It was impressive to watch how fast and skillfully he and the crew shuffled the cars in and out of the industrial sites. NP benefited much from their many satisfied customers.

Bozeman remains one of my favorite places. It's also the home of Rufus Cone, professor of physics at Montana State University, who is a dedicated NP historian. Rufus and his wife, Margaret, have a beautiful residence on the outskirts of town. Looking out their back window yields a marvelous view of fields and mountains—not a building in sight. Another attraction at Bozeman is the Museum of the Rockies, the home of Ronald Nixon's negatives and papers.

7007A
NORTHERN PACIFIC
7007

*Canadian National 6044 at Vancouver, British Columbia, June 15, 1953.*

In recent years, Canada's two transcontinental lines, the Canadian National (the northerly route) and the Canadian Pacific (more to the south), have done a fine job of adding new technology by utilizing heavy ballast and rail, concrete ties, sophisticated dispatching, and the latest in motive power. I was amazed when I first saw a Canadian National conductor step into a wayside building at a division point, enter a code in a fax machine, and immediately receive his orders in big, bold print.

There is little difference between the appearance of trains in Canada and the United States—unit coal and unit grain trains intermingle with container trains. VIA Rail, Canada's version of Amtrak, has been forced to cut back in frequency of schedules, but continues to provide transcontinental service between Vancouver and Toronto three days a week. VIA has not had the funds to purchase new "Superliner"-type cars, but has completely refurbished the passenger cars it received from the CN and CP. These cars are identical to those used on Northern Pacific's Vista-Dome *North Coast Limited* and Great Northern's *Empire Builder*. The unobstructed view of the Canadian Rockies from a dome-car is matchless.

There really is something special about train travel; it's a mix of modern convenience, memories, and mystique.

## *Boxer Jock McOmber, the NP's "Caledonian Clouter."*

For ten years, 1935–45, Brakeman Jock McOmber made headlines in the sports pages the hard way: as a professional light heavyweight boxer. He compiled an amazing record of 38 wins–2 losses, highlighted by two encounters with the nation's tenth-ranked heavyweight at the time, Ernie Collins. They each won one fight and were scheduled for a third, but Collins decided he'd taken enough of Jock's punishment and backed out.

Jock was immensely popular with Tacoma fans, and I can remember bragging to my friends after I went to work for the NP that "I know Jock McOmber."

Ironically, Jock's powerful punching led to his early retirement from boxing. His manager, the legendary Jack Conner, found it increasingly difficult to find opponents willing to battle the "Caledonian Clouter" and bouts became few and far between. The pay wasn't that great, either. Even though Jock had become the Light Heavyweight Champion of the Northwest, the average purse for a fight was only one hundred dollars—a far cry from the big bucks commanded by today's fighters! Jock finally decided to devote himself full time to his first love: railroading. His career spanned almost forty years with the NP and BN.

*NP 2653 at Bismarck, North Dakota, September 13, 1946.*

Ronald Nixon, in his outstanding series of Northern Pacific motive power articles in NP's *Tell Tale* publication, vividly describes witnessing the most dramatic introduction ever given a new locomotive.

> It was at the "Wings of a Century" pageant during the Chicago World Fair in September, 1934. The array of transportation parading across the stage was truly representative of a century of progress. It began with such engines as the Tom Thumb, Pioneer, William Galloway, DeWitt Clinton, Stourbridge Lion and Thomas Jefferson. These patriarchs were followed by the western trail-blazers, among them the Minnetonka, William Crooks and C.P. Huntington. Then came larger and speedier engines—William Mason, Thatcher Perkins and the famous 999 which in 1893 set a world record of 112 miles per hour en route to another Chicago World Fair.
>
> Each succeeding display of larger and more powerful locomotives built up to a climax, which, when it came, was even more dramatic than expected, judging from the reaction of the thousands of spectators. A mammoth, glistening, highwheeled passenger engine which dwarfed all others, moved into the center of the stage, chime whistle blowing and melodious bell ringing. Instead of passing out of sight, as had the others, Northern Pacific Number 2650 stopped in the middle of the stage, amidst the "oh's" and "ah's" of the audience, thereby ending the greatest railroad show of all time.
>
> The 2650 was rushed from the Baldwin Locomotive Works to participate in the Fair. One of ten Class A-2 Northern's, she weighed 877,950 pounds, had a steam pressure of 260 pounds and a tractive effort of 69,800 pounds. The semi-Vanderbilt tank held 20,000 gallons of water and 54,000 pounds of coal, enabling the 77 inch drivers to haul heavy passenger trains at high speed for long distances.

Later in the article, Ronald said, "Their rather unsightly stacks were replaced with extension stacks which could be lowered, permitting them to enter the Twin Cities where overhead clearances are low." I'm afraid I disagree with his opinion about the stacks; I liked the original ones. They were large and had a very noticeable flair. To each his own, I guess.

When I returned home from my first trip to Chicago in 1946, the A-2s had been bumped by diesels from the *North Coast Limited* and relegated to the *Alaskan,* the train I was aboard. The station stop at Bismarck gave me enough time to walk up to the head end and photograph the 2653. I didn't know at the time that engineers would lower the unattractive extension stacks for picture purposes.

2653
2653
2653
2653
2653
NORTHERN PACIFIC

*Two Z-3 compound Mallet engines on westward freight leaving Easton, Washington, May 1943.*

Three of these old compound Mallet engines were needed to boost a full 3,750-ton train over Stampede Pass. One was on the head end to take the train to Auburn, another was ahead of the caboose and was cut off at Stampede, and the rear helper would be cut off on the fly at Martin.

The little, ancient wooden caboose was sandwiched in between the helpers since it couldn't withstand the shove of two of these monsters from behind. The conductor boarded the caboose as the train passed the station gaining speed for the climb. I always marveled at the perfect timing as a conductor caught the grab iron with his hands and swung his legs gracefully up to the steps. Particularly memorable was gangly Conductor Fred W. "Sambo" Sampson, who looked like poetry in motion. Sambo later would lose his life in a caboose in a tragic accident near Steilacoom when his train, First 679, was rear-ended by Great Northern Number 671.

These old Z-3 compound Mallet "Sows," as they were nicknamed, had been struggling up the mountain for thirty years and had only a short time left in their careers. Within a year, sleek, new four-unit diesels would be replacing them. Even though they had served faithfully, no one lamented the passing of the slow, rough-riding Mallets. Company management was particularly pleased—a four-unit diesel road engine with a four-unit helper could take 6,000 tons over the mountain, almost twice as much as the Z-3s.

4014

*"The Viaduct" over the Green River, under construction, 1914.*

Northern Pacific's original main line up the west side of the Cascades kept along the Green River almost to its headwaters. East of Lester, at Weston, there was a tortuous horseshoe curve, marking the beginning of the steepest part of the climb to the Stampede Pass summit. Beginning in 1913–15, the railroad undertook mammoth improvements that included not only double-tracking, but changing the line to eliminate Weston and its loop. The most spectacular feature of this project was a bridge, 1,100 feet long and 163 feet high, spanning both the Green River and the old grade. It was to be known ever after as "The Viaduct." NP Telegrapher Alma Rivett Floberg, who had taken up photography as a hobby, took priceless pictures of the construction. They are now in an album in the collection of her granddaughter, Paula Vernon.

Alma Alice Rivett's seniority date on the Northern Pacific's Seattle (later Tacoma) Division was April 25, 1911. She retired (under her married name, Alma Floberg) on February 28, 1967, after a remarkable 58-year career as a station agent and telegrapher—"brass pounder" in railroad lingo. She actually started railroading in 1909 in North Dakota. Her father had died in 1904, leaving a widow with six children to support. The kids pitched in to help feed the family. Her older sister, Clarissa, learned to telegraph and went to work at Wahpeton for the NP. Soon, Alma was at the station learning the mysteries of Morse, and proved to be an adept student. Before too long, Clarissa accepted a proposal of marriage from an NP lineman named Frank Dawley and she decided to resign.

In the midst of a shortage of telegraphers, the chief dispatcher was not too happy with Clarissa's decision, to which she responded, "How about my sister? She's good on the wire." Alma passed the wire test and went to work that very night at Mapleton, North Dakota, even though she was not quite sixteen. For the next couple of years Alma bounced around on the extra board and, during a slowdown on the NP, worked ten months for the Great Northern. In the meantime, her original NP chief dispatcher had been promoted to superintendent at Seattle. When Frank and Clarissa went to see him during a visit to the West Coast, he talked them into taking jobs on the Cascade Mountain subdivision. Alma accepted an invitation to join them. All three were sent to old Weston for their first assignments.

Alma's biography—written by NP engineer and author, Max King—was featured in the *Tacoma News Tribune*'s Sunday magazine section on July 23, 1967, with a beautiful cover painting by Jack Christensen showing her at a telegraph key. It's a great story. I particularly like the following segment:

> I was curious to know what impact this marvelous little machine had on her everyday mode of living. She said, "I was never alone or lonesome any time I was on duty in some remote station.
>
> "'MORSE' was there in front of me talking to me. There had been times the little maker of dots and dashes had fairly screamed out world shaking news—The sinking of the Lusitania, America enters the War, The Armistice, Lindbergh arrives in Paris." Many telegraphers heard this startling news hours before it became banner headlines in the papers.

*Seven formerly-NP diesels on "The Viaduct," east of Lester, Washington, July 15, 1979.*

The old, abandoned "Weston Loop" grade a couple miles east of Lester, was a fabulous spot to watch and photograph trains. Unfortunately, I discovered it way too late.

My early photographic efforts were severely inhibited by lack of an automobile. I finally scraped together fifty dollars in 1944 and bought a 1933 Studebaker Rockne, but it could barely get me to work, let alone chase a train. It was constantly overheating and I would have to stop by a river to fill a jug with water to quench its thirst. Gasoline became more readily available when the war ended, but then new cars were in short supply. When someone offered me $150 for my Rockne, it was a deal I couldn't refuse. Anyway, by the time I had reliable wheels, steam engines had just about vanished from the scene and I never was able to photograph one on the Viaduct. It would have been spectacular.

Most of my Viaduct shots were taken near the end of the "covered wagon" era (referring to the original freight diesel design). It was remarkable to see seven of them in one consist as late as 1979, but also a bit of a strange feeling; I remembered my wonder at seeing these engines at Easton in 1944, when they were brand new. When I took this photograph, they were old and worn out, soon to be replaced by far superior models. I guess I felt something in common with them.

825
824

BOILER SHOP
1364
NORTHERN PACIFIC
N.P. 1364 S-4

## *NP 1364, a Baldwin Class S-4, in Tacoma, May 29, 1954.*

The Baldwin Locomotive Works built forty "10-wheeler" 4-6-0 locomotives for the Northern Pacific in 1902. Ronald Nixon, in his evaluation of these Class S-4 engines, rated them as just about the most efficient steam locomotives ever built. They were originally Vauclain compounds with double cylinders utilizing steam twice. First service was pulling hot-shot passenger trains, but they were equally efficient on freights. They also were used in helper service over Stampede Pass. Fifteen years later, they were rebuilt into simple engines with inside steam chests and Stephenson valve gear.

The S-4s had remarkable longevity. Most of them were still in active service in the 1950s, although for the last half of their lifespan they were relegated to local, branch line, and work train service. At Tacoma in the 1950s, the 1381 was used occasionally on the connection for the *North Coast Limited*. The S-4s had one distinct advantage over the more modern, super-power engines—they could negotiate the light rail branch lines where the monsters feared to tread. And, according to veteran Engineman Jack Christensen, S-4s were easy engines to fire and run.

In the early 1950s it became increasingly obvious that diesel locomotion was relegating steam engines to the role of museum pieces. NP decided to preserve its steam engine legacy by donating some of these obsolete locomotives to various cities across the system. Class S-4 1300s were considered a good choice for the western half of the road, since they had never been used east of Livingston, Montana. The 1354 was selected for Pasco, 1356 for Missoula, and 1382 for Helena. On June 6, 1954, John MacDonald in the *Tacoma News Tribune* announced the selection for Tacoma:

> Railway locomotives are like horses in a lot of ways. Veteran engineers will tell you that each has its own personality—some are cantankerous, some are sweet and easy to work with.
>
> Unlike horses, though, very few are put out to pasture after their years of service. For most, the scrap heap looms. One notable exception is Northern Pacific Engine 1364.
>
> Engine 1364—after 52 years of service—will be put out to pasture within the next few weeks, and in one of the nicest pastures around. It's going to be put on its own section of track in Point Defiance Park to serve as a reminder in this dieselized era of the glamour and romance of railroading not so many years ago.

On June 26, Tacoma citizens gathered at Point Defiance Park for the dedication. They listened to speeches by the lieutenant governor, the mayor, and various civic dignitaries. Then NP President Robert S. Macfarlane made an eloquent speech and introduced members of his official party: T. J. Kane, W.C. Smith, E.M. Price, H.J. McLain, R.E. Spellmeyer, and J.L. Norton. I was not the only NP cameraman in attendance—Ronald Nixon and Albert Farrow also were there.

The speakers that day had no way to know that the 1364 was not destined to be a permanent reminder to Tacoma of the glorious age of steam. Twenty years later in 1974, it was moved to Tacoma's Nalley Valley to be restored to operating condition, but after the move the funding for this pricey project collapsed. The locomotive subsequently languished in a shed until the late 1980s, when it was moved to a shop in Mineral. Presently it resides in Toppenish, under the tender loving care of Karl Hammerstrom and the Yakima Rail and Steam Museum Association, who have the resources and expertise to have the 1364 "up and running" in the next year or two. The current plan is to run passenger service on their Toppenish, Simcoe and Western Railroad, which once was NP's Simcoe Branch.

## *NP 3100, sold to the Polson Logging Company in 1940.*

On November 8, 1940, NP Mechanical Superintendent J.B. Neish received the following letter from Assistant Vice President (Mechanical) E.L. Grimm:

> Class Z-1 locomotive 3100, now stored serviceable at Wallace, has been sold to the Polson Logging Company for delivery at Moclips, Washington.
>
> We have agreed to convert this locomotive from coal to oil burner before delivery by applying to it the oil burning equipment now at South Tacoma that was removed from snow plow number 10.
>
> Wish you would please arrange by wire for prompt movement of this locomotive from Wallace to South Tacoma, advising shop superintendent McLain and me date it goes forward.

Logging roads with steep grades were inclined to use Shay, Heisler, and Climax geared locomotives, but would occasionally supplement these with second-hand engines from the bigger railroads.

The Mallet-type 3100 with small-diameter drivers was designed for hill climbing, but had been less than a smashing success for the NP. It was one of six Z-1s built by the Baldwin Locomotive Works for NP in 1910 at the cost of $25,560 each. They were used exclusively on the Rocky Mountain Division—on the Coeur d'Alene Branch from St. Regis, Montana, to Wallace, Idaho, and as helpers on the division's various mountain grades. Unfortunately, they were "poor steamers," had a poorly designed valve gear, and had constant maintenance difficulties. Polson paid $10,000 for the 3100, about forty percent of its original cost. A wonderfully detailed description of the Z-1s appears in Larry Schrenk and Bob Frey's book, *Northern Pacific Classic Steam Era*.

On my first visit to the Polson Railroad Camp in 1948, the 3100 was in a shed where it couldn't be photographed. I had better luck the next time I visited, although by then Polson had been taken over by Rayonier, whose name was now on the tender.

3100
RAYONIER

## *British Columbia's Royal Hudson 2860 and NP 924 at Chehalis, Washington, March 20, 1977.*

The Royal Hudson was one of forty-five semi-streamlined engines (numbered 2820 to 2864) built by the Montreal Locomotive Works between 1937 and 1940 for the Canadian Pacific. In 1939, the CP 2850 brought everlasting fame to the entire fleet by pulling King George VI's Royal Train on a 6,000-mile tour across Canada.

The 2860, pictured here, was in passenger train service between Vancouver and Revelstoke until being retired in 1956 after nearly four million miles of service. The 2860 was saved from the scrapper's torch by the Vancouver Railway Museum Association and was restored to working order under the auspices of the Province of British Columbia, now the owner of the engine.

To help celebrate Queen Elizabeth II's Jubilee in 1977, British Columbia sent the Royal Hudson on a goodwill tour to California. When passing through Chehalis, the Royal Hudson met an older and far less glamorous engine, Northern Pacific's 924. The Rogers Locomotive Works built the 924 in 1899 for the St. Paul and Duluth Railroad, which later became part of the NP. The 924 served faithfully in switch service on the West Coast for many years until finally being sold to the Inland Empire Paper Company in Spokane.

After its career of switching at that plant was over, the 924 was donated to the Puget Sound Railway Historical Association in Snoqualmie, and temporarily placed in storage at the Chehalis Industrial Park in the early 1970s. This was a stroke of good luck for the 924, because there it was fully restored to working order under the tender care of Harold Borovec, a Chehalis fuel dealer with a deep background in railroading. Harold had learned about steam engines "inside-out" by serving as hostler helper, boilermaker helper, and machinist's helper at the Centralia Roundhouse, starting in 1943. Harold's uncle, B.L. Morris, was a veteran NP engineer.

After returning from a year and a half stint in the Navy during WWII, Harold decided to try a different line of railroad work as clerk at Raymond, Winlock, Chehalis, and Centralia. Eventually, he left the railroad for the fuel business in 1958, but his hand remained on the steam locomotive throttle for railfans. He serves as an engineer for the Chehalis-Centralia Road and the Mount Rainier Scenic Railroad—all of which led to the brief but historic meeting of the Royal Hudson and the 924 in March 1977.

2860
BRITISH COLUMBIA
CANADA
924
NORTHERN PACIFIC

*Chehalis Western train on Burlington Northern (formerly NP) South Bend Branch at Meskill Pit on a misty morning, September 18, 1975.*

Lewis and Pacific counties in Washington have a complex railroading history. The Northern Pacific was the first road to span the counties from Chehalis Junction to South Bend, but this line had a prior name of the Yakima and Pacific Coast and also was part of the United Railroads of Washington in its early days. The Chicago, Milwaukee and St. Paul also owned track from Chehalis to Raymond, which likewise had different early names—the Pacific and Eastern and the Puget Sound and Willapa Harbor.

In addition, there were a number of logging railroads, notably the Chehalis Western, owned by the Weyerhaeuser Timber Company. Logging operations shifted as trees were cut, resulting in train service revisions involving both the NP and Milwaukee. Chehalis Western operated over both of these roads, as well as its own, in the service of Weyerhaeuser.

In 1936, for some odd reason, the Milwaukee Road abandoned 18 miles of line from Chehalis to Dryad Junction and commenced operating over NP rails for this portion of the run to Raymond. Chehalis Western then bought 9 miles of Milwaukee track from Chehalis to Ruth.

Once I was called to work at the South Bend Branch. While working day shift at Easton I was told to report the next day at Millburn, a small station 6 miles west of Chehalis, where Chehalis Western trains entered the NP. Since I didn't own an automobile, after work that day I boarded Number 5 at Easton for East Auburn and caught the connection to Tacoma. From Tacoma, I took the "Owl," Number 402, at 1:15 A.M. and arrived in Chehalis at 3:25 A.M. Unfortunately, no one had told me how to find Millburn. The night clerk at Chehalis had never heard of Millburn, and the yardmaster whom I phoned at Centralia couldn't tell me how to get there.

Finally, I called a taxi and the driver was able to find the dirt road to the station. I immediately contacted Weyerhaeuser and was informed that their trains would not be running that day. When I telegraphed this information to the NP dispatcher in Tacoma, he said that I wouldn't be needed and could go home! Luckily, I had asked the taxi to stand by; I had been alerted that this might happen. Never had I expended so much effort to do so little.

Over the years I had the good fortune to make a number of trips by train over the South Bend Branch. The track followed the tree-lined Chehalis River most of the way and the fall foliage was breathtaking. There were a number of good photo locations and I particularly liked this one at Meskill Pit.

684
684
684
CHEHALIS
WESTERN

684
684
684
684
5602
5602
THE MILWAUKEE ROAD
306-RS

## *Curtis, Millburn and Eastern 684 and Milwaukee 5602 at Chehalis, 1976.*

In the mid-1970s, Weyerhaeuser converted the southernmost 10 miles of its Chehalis Western Railroad into a common carrier, called the Curtis, Millburn and Eastern. Curtis was more-or-less at the end of a 9-mile stretch of track purchased from the Milwaukee in 1938. The intent in 1975 was to build a mill at Curtis and earn revenue on carloads shipped all across the United States after interchanging to one of the class one roads at Chehalis. The mill never was built, but a log yard was established.

When the Milwaukee folded in 1980, Weyerhaeuser acquired the Milwaukee's Chehalis to Tacoma line, originally named the Tacoma Eastern. The former name Chehalis Western was resurrected and its crews handled log trains all the way from Chehalis to Tacoma. In 1992, Weyerhaeuser discontinued handling logs by rail in this area. The company turned the line over to the City of Tacoma in 1994 and now it is part of the Tacoma Rail Division of the city's Public Utilities Department.

In 1976, when this picture was taken at Chehalis, no one realized that the end was so near. Today, both the Milwaukee line to Raymond and NP's South Bend Branch have been abandoned and the rails taken up. Chehalis Western and Curtis, Millburn and Eastern trains no longer run.

One sparkling jewel remains. Harold Borovec and his associates formed the Chehalis-Centralia Railroad Association and began running a steam excursion train from Chehalis to Curtis on the former Chehalis Western track, which is now owned by the Port of Chehalis. Their beautiful Mikado-type 2-8-2 locomotive is the former Cowlitz, Chehalis and Cascade 15. It's a delightful trip, running on weekends from March through September.

## *Class Z-3 Mallet 4005 at Wymer, Washington, May 20, 1944.*

Class Z-3 Mallet 4005 on a westbound "dead freight" (i.e., a low-priority load, such as lumber, grain, coal, etc.) is getting a drink of water at Wymer while waiting on the siding for hot-shot freight Number 602 to pass by. Wymer was just 20 miles north of Yakima, where the train started. Seventeen miles beyond Wymer, at Ellensburg, 4005 would need another drink. Upon arriving at Cle Elum, 4005 would be hungry, so its coal tender would be filled there. At Easton, there would be another water stop.

No wonder diesel engines had such an edge in operating efficiency! They had no need to stop anywhere over a division for fuel or water.

Just behind the fireman on the 4005's tender is a protrusion called the "doghouse." A Z-3 engine had only enough room in the cab to seat the engineer and fireman. The little structure at the rear of the tender was provided for the head brakeman. I rode in a Z-3's doghouse once from Martin to Yakima. I had worked all night and was trying to sleep, but this little shack was most uncomfortable. It seemed to accentuate the rough ride of the Z-3. I remember the rhythmic thumping of my head against the wall as we bounced along.

NORTHERN PACIFIC
11949

*Pasco-Pendleton Local hauling grain, August 5, 1953.*

Hauling grain from Central Washington and the Midwest to the Pacific Coast was a big moneymaking operation for the Northern Pacific. Today, grain is loaded in jumbo, covered hopper cars; but before 1967, forty-foot, single-door B-2 boxcars were the standard conveyance, as seen in this photo of the Pasco-Pendleton Local in 1953.

Before being sent out for loading, boxcars had to be "coopered" (i.e., have all cracks caulked). This was done by stuffing rags or stapling heavy paper over potential leaks and then installing grain doors. Grain doors consisted of 1" x 6" and 1" x 8" boards nailed together across the 6' wide doorway, leaving enough room at the top to pour in the grain.

When the loaded cars arrived at a grain elevator, the door boards were removed and the cars were tilted and shaken to empty the grain into underground pits. Today's covered hoppers have eliminated the need to shake the cars. Roof hatches counter a vacuum effect when the gates underneath the hopper cars are opened to let gravity do its thing.

1362
NORTHERN PACIFIC
1362
NP

NORTHERN
PACIFIC

## *First Tacoma Division diesel, Class FT 6001, at Wymer, Washington, May 19, 1944.*

Class FT 6001 was the first road diesel to enter service on the Tacoma Division and had been around only a month when this picture was taken at Wymer. The white flags on the front of the engine indicate that the train is running as an "Extra" and was not listed in the operating time table. The factory had installed the flag brackets just below the engineer and fireman's windows. However, they proved to be prone to snagging train orders from hoops, so a modification was made soon afterwards to move the brackets to a position above the windows.

An old refrigerator car is located on the left. Because summers were miserably hot in the Yakima River canyon, the company provided ice for the employees at Wymer. Visible on the right is a footbridge across the river that provided access to the highway and the outside world.

*NP's streamliner test train between Black River and Argo, Washington, November 4, 1946.*

"Sails in on Wings of Wind" was the caption for the Seattle *Post-Intelligencer* photo of NP's streamliner test train when it arrived at King Street Station on November 4, 1946, shortly after I took this picture.

Northwest railroads had placed orders for new, streamlined passenger cars to be built as soon as possible after the end of World War II. It didn't take long for production to get into full swing and NP started receiving the first of its new cars a little more than a year after the war was over.

NP decided to operate a test train with some of the new cars to see how they would react at various speeds, as well as to determine the most practical schedule for a speedy upgrade of the *North Coast Limited*. The train departed St. Paul November 2, consisting of a three-unit diesel locomotive, dynamometer car, baggage car, seven new coaches, and three business cars. There were only railroad officials aboard, plus Douglass Welch, columnist for the Seattle *P-I,* who was a rail buff with a great sense of humor. He was accompanied (in his own words) by "Mr. I.W. Harper [a bourbon whiskey], a convivial soul, who is helping us write in the secretary's office on NP President C.E. Denny's car at the end of the train." Welch filed reports of the run as the train progressed. The following are some of his observations:

> St. Paul, Minn., Nov. 2
>
> This train at this moment is champing at the bit in the lower yards, all 4,500 horses of its horsepower, and there is such an air of anxious waiting and expectancy and so much tension in the atmosphere that if you were to say "boo" to the engineer he would be halfway to Minneapolis before you got it all out.
>
> Mr. Denny is looking at his watch now, and so are half a dozen other officials, and Mr. Harper seems slowly to have evaporated away into nothingness. From here to the coast everyone on this railway has an eye on this train.
>
> Livingston, Mont., Nov. 3
>
> This was supposed to be pretty much of a secret, this test run. There was very little advance publicity, except in that big blabbermouth of a paper, The *P-I* in Seattle. News services must have picked it up in Seattle and funneled it back here, because thousands of people lined the railway in Minnesota, North Dakota and Montana to watch us pass.
>
> Butte, Mont., Nov. 3
>
> After attaining a speed of 91 miles an hour for a few minutes west of Story, Montana, the big 4,500 horsepower diesel-electric engine unaided hauled her 850-ton train up a 2.2 percent grade at a uniform speed of 28 MPH. This was the first time, testing officials said, that a passenger locomotive hauled a train of such tonnage over Butte Mountain without the assistance of a helper engine.
>
> Final report from Seattle Nov. 4
>
> Jack rabbits looked like they were standing still in eastern Washington…
>
> In Lester, the children hung out of the windows of their school and waved us madly on…
>
> We came down through Auburn and Kent and Black River at a uniform 80 MPH; and the grade crossings everywhere were black and blurred with masses of people who had turned out to watch us pass. We came out faster than any train has run before from St. Paul to Seattle—34 hours and 34 minutes.

All of this turned out to be "much ado about nothing," because six months later NP had a complete reversal of policy. On May 3, 1947, President Denny announced that fast trains on the Great Northern and Milwaukee would be enough for the Northwest and NP was withdrawing. But, thankfully, another reversal came in 1952 when NP jumped back in with the accelerated "Faster" *North Coast Limited.*

754

6500

## *No. 26, the faster "North Coast Limited," November 18, 1952, at Kanaskat, Washington.*

Most of my career in the Tacoma Dispatchers' Office was spent on third trick, the midnight to 8:00 A.M. "graveyard" shift. A nightly routine, when time permitted, involved checking the chief dispatcher's "In Basket" to see what was new. Just about the all-time greatest thrill in my tenure with the railroad occurred one night in the summer of 1952 as I read the latest notice. Out of the blue, from the president of the road, it came as a huge surprise to read:

> TO NORTHERN PACIFIC EMPLOYEES
>
> It is with great satisfaction and pride that I report to you an important step forward by the Northern Pacific.
>
> On Sunday, November 16, the North Coast Limited will go on a new fast schedule between Chicago, the Twin Cities and the North Pacific Coast that will save travelers 12 hours westbound and 9½ hours eastbound.
>
> On the same day, we will put in service a second transcontinental train called The Main Streeter, which will operate on approximately the present schedule of the North Coast Limited.
>
> Also, our board of directors has authorized an expenditure of $5,800,000 for new equipment which includes 16 Vista-Dome cars for the North Coast Limited. This equipment will be ordered very shortly, although of course it will be many months before it can be delivered.
>
> The new time of the North Coast Limited will be 46½ hours between Chicago and Seattle.
>
> Public announcement of our new passenger service will be made in next Sunday's newspapers. Until then, please keep this information to yourselves. After that, I hope you will do everything you can to bring the information to the attention of the public and recommend NP service to your friends, relatives and people with whom you do business.
>
> The new service and the new equipment will cost your company a lot of money and we need all the business we can get to make it pay.
>
> I know I can count on your full co-operation.
>
> Robert S. Macfarlane,
> President

Wow! Northern Pacific passenger service had taken a back seat to the Great Northern and Milwaukee Road after World War II. All three roads had ordered and received new streamlined equipment but NP elected to remain on a slower schedule, mixing old cars with new ones. Now we were jumping to the forefront—with Vista Dome cars like icing on the cake! The cooperation President Macfarlane asked for was gladly given because now we could feel that no road had a better train than ours.

I was on hand at East Auburn with my camera on November 16 to photograph the first run of the faster *North Coast Limited.* My good friend Ed Foisie was the engineer and the Auburn Roundhouse Drum and Bugle Corps was on hand to serenade the large crowd assembled to see this wonderful train.

Two days later, on my day off, I went to Kanaskat where there was a picturesque curve to photograph the new streamliner.

## *General Motors Electro-Motive "Aerotrain" at Tacoma, April 1956.*

In the 1950s, there was a wide variation in passenger service policy among the nation's railroads. Some allowed their trains to deteriorate with the hope that patronage would disappear and passenger operations could be discontinued. Others, particularly those with a strong passenger service tradition, endeavored to be innovative and sought exotic ways to attract the traveling public. General Motors, with its eye on the railroad market, introduced several experimental concepts with the hope of coming up with a design that would catch on and be a sales success. One of these was the Aerotrain, which was described in a brochure titled, "Here Comes Tomorrow—A New Concept in Passenger Train Travel":

> The new lightweight Aerotrain, developed by Electro-Motive Division of General Motors, points the way to hitherto unequalled standards of speed, comfort and economy in train travel. This 10-coach experimental train incorporates a new concept in integrated design of Diesel motive power and cars, with Air Suspension springing, to give passengers a smoother ride at sustained speeds of 100 miles an hour.
>
> It is General Motors' answer to the railroads' need for passenger-hauling equipment that will reduce capital investment and cost less to operate and maintain.

Two demonstrator train sets were built, with one going to the Pennsylvania Railroad and the other making a whirlwind tour of the New York Central, Santa Fe, and Union Pacific. (The latter had it at the time this photo was taken.)

Critics claimed it was a feeble attempt by General Motors to create a market for its intercity buses, because the trains were made from bus components. The cars were flimsy and uncomfortable, and were said to ride like a runaway stagecoach. Apparently the criticisms were valid, as both sets were returned to General Motors and no more were built. A home was found for the two demonstrator sets on the Rock Island Railroad, but after a few years in commuter service they were scrapped.

A scaled-down Aerotrain replica can be seen in Portland on the Washington Park and Zoo Railway.

## *Fireman grabbing train orders at UP Junction (Tacoma), October 26, 1969.*

They handed him his orders at Monroe, Virginia,
Saying "Steve, you are way behind time,
This is not 38 but it's old 97
You must put her into Spencer on time."

The "Wreck of the Old 97," though one of my favorite railroad ballads, gives an inaccurate picure of train orders. Train orders were written instructions a centrally located dispatcher dictated by telephone or Morse code to operators at wayside stations, who would transcribe and deliver them to trains, usually "on the fly." In this photo, the fireman grabs his train orders from a clip on the forked "hoop." This system was initiated in the 1850s and remained in use until finally being phased out by signal and radio systems in the 1980s. The irony had hit me when Neil Armstrong landed on the moon in 1969: we had the technology to put men on the moon, but still were controlling trains with pieces of paper!

There were specific types of orders, all prescribed by the Consolidated Code of Operating Rules. For example, if a scheduled train was running late, a dispatcher could notify inferior trains by either giving an order providing them with later times at stations en route, or one that would state, for example, "Number 408 run 30 minutes late Centralia to Vancouver."

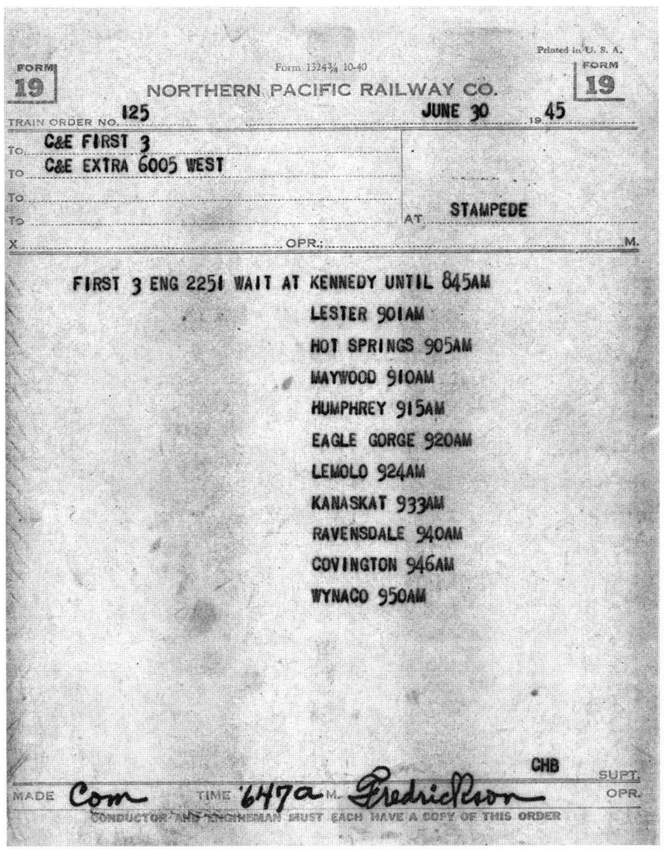
Printed in U. S. A.
FORM 19 Form 1324¾ 10-40 FORM 19
NORTHERN PACIFIC RAILWAY CO.
TRAIN ORDER NO. 125 JUNE 30 1945
TO C&E FIRST 3
TO C&E EXTRA 6005 WEST
TO
TO AT STAMPEDE
X OPR. M.

FIRST 3 ENG 2251 WAIT AT KENNEDY UNTIL 845AM
LESTER 901AM
HOT SPRINGS 905AM
MAYWOOD 910AM
HUMPHREY 915AM
EAGLE GORGE 920AM
LEMOLO 924AM
KANASKAT 933AM
RAVENSDALE 940AM
COVINGTON 946AM
WYNACO 950AM

CHB SUPT.
MADE Com TIME 647a M. Fredrickson OPR.
CONDUCTOR AND ENGINEMAN MUST EACH HAVE A COPY OF THIS ORDER

On a single track, to establish meeting or passing points, orders would read: "Number 2 meet Number 1 at Eagle Gorge" or "Number 25 pass Number 1 at Ellensburg."

"Extra" trains, those not scheduled in the operating time tables, needed an order giving them permission to proceed. It could not be issued until provisions were made for meeting opposing extra trains. (These trains were obliged to clear the time of scheduled trains.)

Then there were "slow" orders, notifying trains of track conditions slowing train movement. There were a variety of other forms of orders for specific situations, but there was a definite *absence* of an order to an engineer to get his train "in on time." I learned this by experience. One evening at Martin, early in my career, I knew the dispatcher was eager to get a helper engine cutting off from an eastbound train back to Lester for the next train. So I informed the crew, "The dispatcher wants you to hurry down to Lester." After I proudly related my train message to the dispatcher, he thoroughly chastised me for giving a message that might induce the crew to exceed the speed limit. I learned my lesson.

*A copy of train orders signed by Jim Fredrickson, June 30, 1945, at Stampede.*

6702C
6702C F

## *Easton Station, June 15, 1970.*

While attending the University of Puget Sound, my son Tim worked as a relief operator for two summers. One of his first assignments was Easton. On a sunny day in July, my wife Cereta and I drove up for a visit in our 1968 Dodge Dart, which is parked on the platform. That's Tim holding up the hoop with orders for an approaching train. Most memories of Easton are pleasant, but the speeder at the west end of the station brings back one that still makes me shudder after 56 years.

In June 1945, I had been sent to Stampede to work third trick until further notice. On arrival I found a vacant little room adjoining the telegraph office that could serve nicely as a photo darkroom. So, on my next day off I went home and returned with my picture-making equipment, including the rather bulky enlarger. I didn't have a car at the time so I must have loaded it all on Number 4. Before long I was busily producing pictures. Then, without warning, I received a message from the chief dispatcher telling me I was done at Stampede and would commence second trick at Easton the next day.

At midnight, after finishing my first shift at Easton, I was lamenting out loud that I had left my enlarger behind at Stampede—how was I going to retrieve it? Night Roundhouse Foreman Doug Gordon, in the office at the time, overheard me and said, "No problem. Water Service Foreman Joe Pratt's speeder is in the warehouse—just take it, run up to Stampede, load your enlarger, and bring it back here." I tried to explain that I knew nothing about running a speeder, but Doug wouldn't take no for an answer. He said that he would show me how. We dragged it out to the westward track and started the engine. He pointed to one lever, saying "That makes it go," and to another saying, "That makes it stop."

So away I went, very nervous at first, but before long I seemed to get the hang of it and started feeling more comfortable. It was a pitch black night and I remember the headlight shining on deer bounding across the track just ahead of me. I successfully arrived at Martin, got the staff for permission to go through the big tunnel, and in short time was loading my belongings aboard at Stampede. Then it was through the tunnel again and down the eastward track from Martin.

Then came, without a doubt, the *dumbest* thing I ever did in my entire railroad career. Double track ends at Easton and there was a spring switch going onto single track. The switch was normally lined for westward movements up the westward track. For eastward trains the spring switch points would move as the wheels went through, making it unnecessary to stop and line the switch. The motor car setoff was off the westward track so I reasoned—smart fellow that I was—why not run through the spring switch and come back to the station on the westward?

There was one snag to my plan. Heavy engine wheels activate the spring switch, but little, light speeder wheels don't. I unceremoniously derailed on the switch. When I looked down the track to the east, sure enough, I could see the headlight of an approaching engine in the distance. I made a dash for the nearby roundhouse office and found Doug, snoozing on a table. I shook him and screamed, "I'm on the ground and there's a train coming!" He didn't respond and I ran back to the speeder. Soon it dawned on Doug what I had just yelled at him and he followed right on my tail. The two of us rolled the speeder off the track just before the train roared by. If it'd been a few seconds later, my railroad career would have come to an inglorious end.

For years afterward, whenever I saw Doug he would start laughing before even a word was spoken.

EASTON

## *Retirement party, November 1959.*

My vote for the all-time best master-of-ceremonies for retirement parties goes to Superintendent Worthington C. Smith, shown here standing between Clementina and Sam Campanelli. Smith's great sense of humor at the Campanellis' retirement dinner made the evening relaxed, enjoyable, and fun for all, as the smiles show.

Smith described his railroad career as "very uninteresting," but few "rails" were assigned to such a variety of positions and locations as he was. Starting as a brakeman in Canada, he next worked for the Northern Pacific as brakeman on the Tacoma Division. After that, he became secretary to the superintendent, transferred to the Traffic Department in Portland, and later returned to the Operating Department as trainmaster—first in Spokane, and then Billings. He served in World War I, and again in World War II with the Railway Operating Battalion in Persia and western Europe. He returned to the NP in 1945 as trainmaster at Billings, and then Missoula. He was promoted to superintendent, Lake Superior Division, at Duluth in 1950, and came to Tacoma as superintendent in 1954, where he retired in 1961. To paraphrase Will Rogers, "I never worked for a superintendent I didn't like, and Worthington Smith was one of the most likable."

Sam Campanelli and his wife, Clementina, were high on my list of likable people. Sam immigrated from Loseta, Italy, around the turn of the century, when he was eighteen. He first worked in logging camps—not the most pleasant places to be in 1901—until starting with the NP as a section man, where he was later promoted to foreman. He served as foreman at Stampede for nineteen years. It is hard to imagine that working in a logging camp could be tougher than battling winter snows at Stampede Pass.

In Sam's era, huge mechanized track gangs had not yet appeared on the scene. Instead, there were small section crews for about every ten miles of track. Besides Sam, other foremen I remember during my time on the "Mountain" were Miguel Ambriz at Covington, Mike Mola at Ravensdale, George Galimanis at Kanaskat, Joe DeVito at Humphrey, Pucci Sabatino at Lester, Vito Ferri at Martin, Dominic Abinanti at Easton, Vito Petrelli at Cle Elum, Joe Pannatoni at Thorp, George Kontos at Ellensburg, O.L. Franz at Wymer, Tom Monacelli at Selah, and Louis Gagoush at Yakima.

The track supervisors I knew in those days were Fred Kristfelt east of Cle Elum, and Matt Fioretti to the west. Riding down the "Mountain" with Matt on his speeder was an unforgettable experience. We went so fast it seemed like the wheels hit only about every third rail. J.O. Davies was roadmaster at Lester. He later became superintendent at Tacoma and eventually vice president of the Billings Region for the BN. Gus Kavadias, Joe Pipkin, and Harvey Armes followed him at Lester before the roadmaster position was phased out. Alva Gerdon was the first trainmaster I knew on the "Mountain." Jerry Bergman and Bob Robey were famous for their skill at snow fighting when they served as trainmaster and roadmaster, respectively.

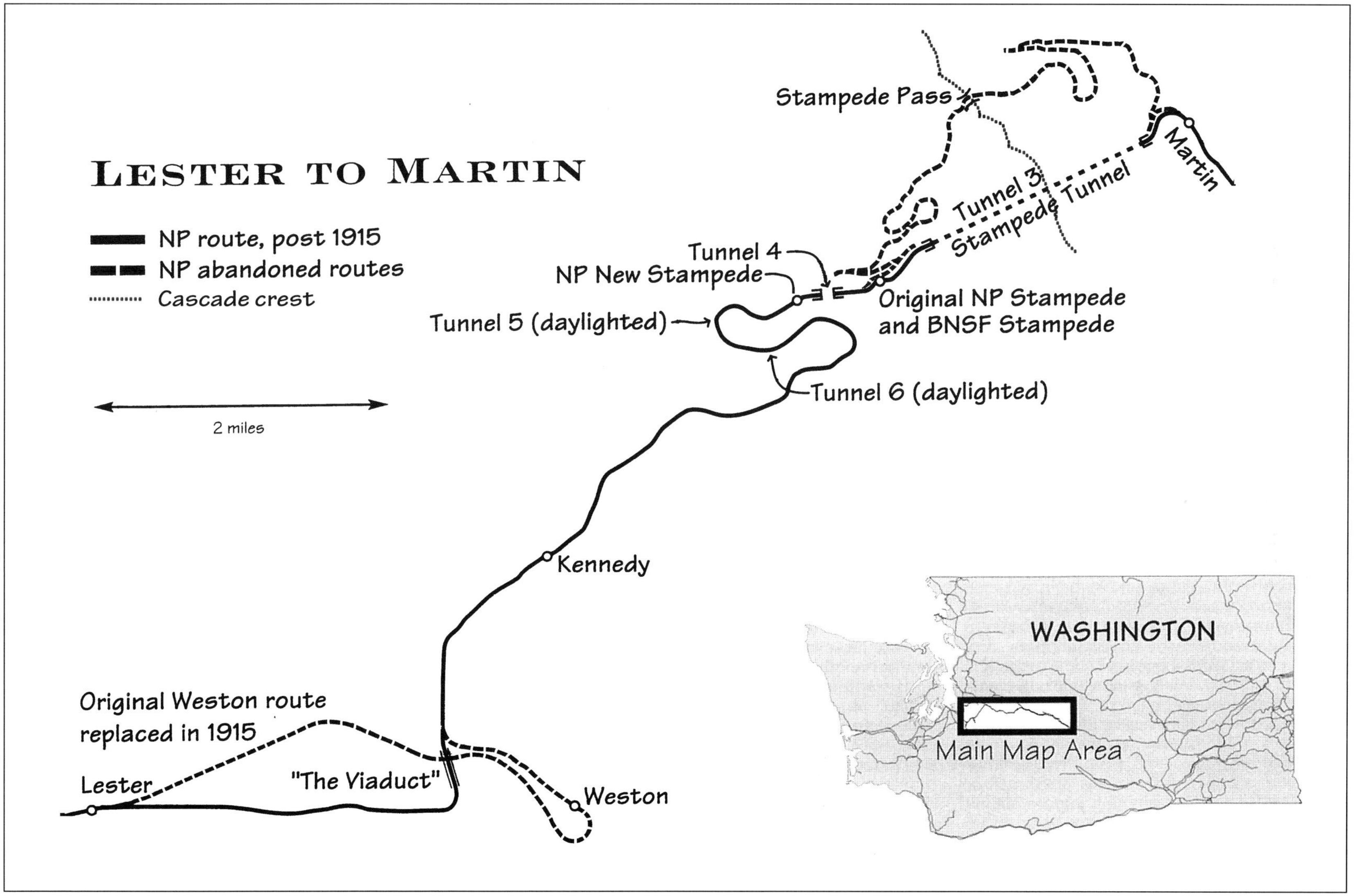


Map courtesy of CTC Board Railroads Illustrated

## *View from the "North Coast Limited" passing under the Milwaukee overhead near Easton, March 12, 1963.*

In this scene, the *North Coast Limited* passes under the Milwaukee overhead crossing just west of Easton and will continue along the Yakima River for the next two hours. During WWII, I heard someone offer the opinion that this would be a strategic spot for an enemy air raid, knocking out two vital railroads with one bomb.

Ahead on the left is what geologists call the Roslyn formation. In the 1990s, the town of Roslyn became the location of a popular television series, *Northern Exposure*. This little town just north of Cle Elum enjoyed its time in the limelight under the dramatized name of Cicely, Alaska, home of characters Joel, Maggie, and their cohorts. So many tourists came to see the location of the popular show that there were weekend traffic jams in Roslyn.

This was the kind of trip I really enjoyed in the good old NP days. It was nice to see friends like Harold Nordgren, the conductor that day, and Henry Gupton, one of the many expert engineers that NP was fortunate to have. It was hard to decide just where to ride on this magnificent train. There were two vista-dome cars out of Seattle and two more from Portland that were added at Pasco. There was no better way to view the scenery than from a seat in the dome. But then there was the fascinating Lewis and Clark Traveler's Rest Car, decorated to honor the famous expedition, where food and drink were available as well as opportunity to get acquainted with fellow passengers from all over the world. People with Pullman sleeping car accommodations had the privilege of riding in the observation-lounge, the last car in the train, and watching the scenic countryside fly by. Of course, at mealtime there was no question where to sit. "Nothing could be finer than dinner in the diner" on the NP, that always included the famed "great big" baked potato.

I liked taking photographs from a vestibule near the rear, with the upper half of the dutch door open. That's where I stood to take this photo. These days, the railroads are safety sensitive, and opening these doors is forbidden.

*Hotel Easton, June 15, 1944.*

There is not much left around Easton to commemorate its prominent role in Northern Pacific history. Pacific railroad explorers George McClellan and Abiel Tinkham camped in the vicinity in the 1850s and E.L. McGinnis homesteaded about a mile east of the present townsite before the railroad arrived in 1886. McGinnis built a 12-room hotel in anticipation of the railroad and its travelers and workers, expecting to have a station and town established on his property. However, NP officials didn't like the high price he was asking and located their facilities on railroad land about a mile to the west.

Easton was the east side counterpart to the helper station on the other side of the Cascades at Weston. The coming of the Chicago, Milwaukee and Puget Sound Railway (Milwaukee Road) through Easton in the early 1900s brought a boom to Easton—particularly in saloons, with 12 springing up. In 1907, a fire destroyed all but one, but they were quickly rebuilt. In 1913, another disastrous fire again reduced them to ashes, along with most of the business district, including the hotel. No one stepped in to rebuild the hotel, creating a major dilemma for the NP to accommodate its helper crews and temporary workers, particularly in the winter when snow plow crews needed housing. Finally in 1917, NP officials decided to convert a run-down, old, section-worker bunkhouse into a hotel. Section Foreman Matthew Perdang and his wife signed a contract with the railroad to operate and maintain the upgraded property.

Originally, the hotel included a kitchen and dining room. By the 1940s when I came to work at Easton, the hotel no longer provided food service. There was no 24-hour restaurant in town and with a daily need to feed not only local railroaders but also freight train crews, the company tried to provide food service in an old dining car that was set on a spur. The solution was short-lived, as the place earned a reputation for serving up too many cases of food poisoning, blamed by its patrons on the ever-changing, itinerant cooks. Finally, Mrs. Dave McPhee, wife of one of the locomotive engineers, opened her home for boarding-house style meals. Because she was an outstanding cook, eating at Easton became a gourmet treat.

*Diagram of staff machine.*

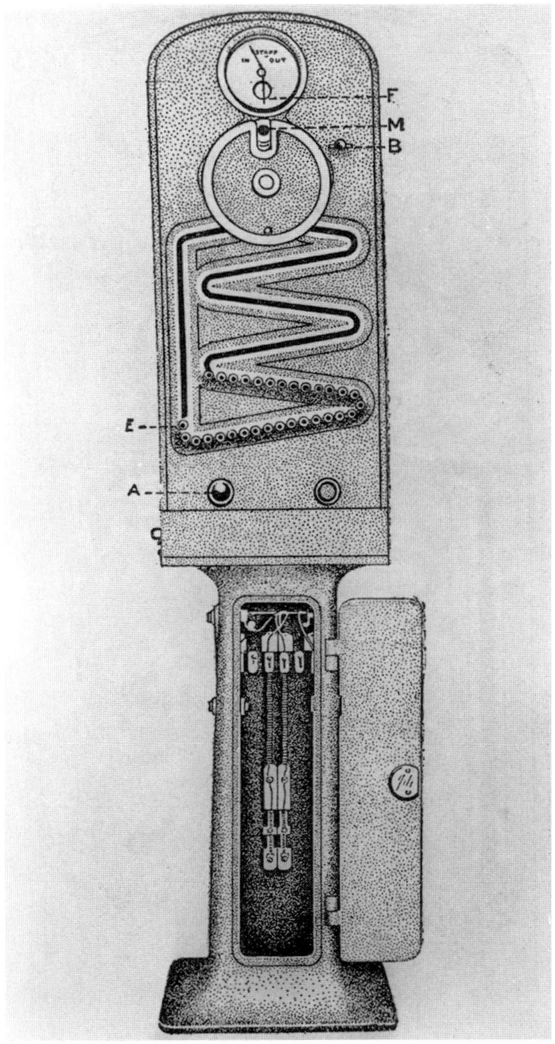


"Northern Pacific Special Instructions" gave a clear, concise description of the staff system used to ensure that there wouldn't be more than one train at a time between Stampede and Martin.

> No train, engine or self-propelled car will run in either direction until engineman receives from operator a staff which must be retained and delivered to the operator at the opposite end of the block.
>
> The possession of the staff makes the train superior to all other trains between Stampede and Martin. The eastward train order signal at Stampede, and westward train order signal at Martin, are interlocked with staff machines in the telegraph office at Stampede and Martin, and except when used must be set normally at stop and cannot be cleared until operator at opposite end of block returns staff to machine. After signal has been cleared for a train entering the tunnel it must be restored to stop immediately after the rear of the train has passed the signal.

The staff was a round, metallic plug six inches long and three-fourths of an inch in diameter with a series of indentations somewhat like a key. The lever to clear the train order signal could not be moved without being unlocked by the staff.

In the diagram, the staffs can be seen at the bottom of the zig-zag track. To extricate one, the operator punched the button marked "A" three times, which rang a bell on the other machine at the opposite end of the Stampede Tunnel. The releasing operator would hold down on his button while his counterpart would move a staff up the track to the revolving, round metal plate. The staff would be moved into the indentation on this plate, revolved to the top, and extricated. The operator next placed the staff in a container on a hoop and delivered it to the engineer of a train entering the tunnel, who would throw it off at the other end. Both machines were dead until the staff was replaced.

Each machine contained about 30 staffs. The only person with a key to open a machine was the signal maintainer. If a preponderance of trains in one direction caused an accumulation of too many staffs on one end of the system, he would open the overloaded machine, remove some of the staffs, and take them to the other device. This action was known as "balancing the staffs."

On very rare occasions an engineer would forget to throw off the staff and take it through to Easton or Lester. When this happened, the staff system was temporarily taken out of service and complicated train orders were used instead.

In 1957, the staff system was replaced by centralized traffic control signals with a machine at Easton operated by the telegrapher under the direction of the dispatcher in Tacoma. The stations at Stampede and Martin then were closed.

## *East portal of Tunnel 4 at Stampede Pass.*

There originally were eight tunnels on the Northern Pacific route between Ellensburg and Auburn. Here is a historic photo of one of only two tunnels that remain today, both of which are at the summit of Stampede Pass. The more famous of the two is the 9,834-foot-long Tunnel 3, which has the route's crest near its center. A mile to its west is Tunnel 4, only 650 feet long but ruggedly spectacular, particularly at the east portal. When the second track was installed between Lester and Easton in 1914, it ended at the west portal of this tunnel and resumed again three miles to the east at Martin, on the eastern end of Tunnel 3. The other six tunnels were eliminated by line changes or daylighting.

The original Stampede telegraph office was located a little to the east of where this photo was taken. In 1914, a new station called New Stampede was built at the west end of Tunnel 4 where the new switch from double to single track was located. The older station between the tunnels became Old Stampede, which was converted to living quarters for the day telegrapher and day vent plant operator.

Not too much has changed in the many years since this construction-era photo was taken. Many of the trees are gone and a power-line tower is a modern addition, but the rock formations look the same. The promontory at the top is my all-time favorite spot to watch and photograph trains. It's a breathtaking panorama from up there. Looking to the south one can watch trains all the way around NP's big horseshoe curve, the Borup Loop. Toward the west, trains can be viewed making a second hairpin turn to come up to the end of the double track and Tunnel 4. To the east is a view of the track exiting the east side of Tunnel 4, proceeding through Old Stampede, and around a curve just before entering the long Tunnel 3.

I worked and lived just to the west of Tunnel 4 at New Stampede. One night on my trick, about 3:00 A.M., a westbound train threw off a note that a timber was hanging down from the snow shed at the east entrance of Tunnel 4. I called section foreman Sam Campanelli on our local message phone and he appeared shortly with a ladder. He asked me to accompany him and hold his lantern while he climbed up to inspect the situation. As soon as he touched it, the big timber fell, brushing me on its way down. If I had been another inch or two closer I would have been flattened.

Two trains, Number 4 and Number 5, stopped at Old Stampede, located between the two tunnels. During the winter, the floor of Tunnel 4 became a sheet of ice, making it extremely difficult to keep one's footing when walking through it. I usually carried our sturdy two-year-old, Jim, on my shoulders when walking through the tunnel to catch a train to town, but that became impossible due to the slippery conditions. Consequently, I made an appeal to the chief dispatcher to allow a special stop for us at New Stampede. He gave permission, provided we didn't abuse the privilege.

Riding on an eastbound steam engine through Tunnel 4 was unforgettable. It was like being thrown into a furnace. The sudden blast of hot air was much more intense than in the longer Tunnel 3. Perhaps this was because the engine had to work harder in the short tunnel and the grade eased off before trains went into Tunnel 3.

## *NP 6506 at New Stampede, September 15, 1949.*

I loved living at Stampede Pass, surrounded by mountains, forests, wild animals, and (generally) peaceful tranquillity.

In the fall of 1949, I "bid in" third trick at the Stampede station, the midnight to 8:00 A.M. shift. Our underlying goal in moving there from Auburn was financial stability: the company provided housing, fuel, and utilities. The third trick living quarters consisted of three rooms in the back half of the depot, known as New Stampede, at the end of the double track from Lester just before short Tunnel Number 4. The other telegraphers, the section crew, and vent plant operators all lived at Old Stampede, about a half mile away between Tunnel 4 and long Tunnel 3.

It was definitely a different way of life. Second trick operator Herbert "Denny" Denzene would wake me about 15 minutes before midnight. I would come out in my pajamas, sign the transfer, and give the dispatcher a weather report. Number 2, the *North Coast Limited,* was due at 12:28 A.M. and, still in my pj's, I would "hoop up" the staff and respirators to its crew before going back to my quarters and getting dressed.

Once, after a long freight train passed by, I noticed a family of deer standing on the opposite side of the track. The refrigerator cars with ice and salt in their bunkers would drip salt on the ties and the deer enjoyed licking it.

To dispose of garbage we would just throw it over the bank across the tracks from the depot. Then we could watch below as bears rummaged through it for something tasty. They occasionally paused, looked up, and circled their noses. Their eyesight was poor, but they had a keen sense of smell and could usually detect people nearby.

Once I encountered a bear that wasn't paying much attention. It came bounding down the hillside onto the track right near me. For a moment we looked at each other face to face and then we both ran in opposite directions.

City life would never compare to living at Stampede.

It was at Stampede that I witnessed for the first time a diesel helper on Number 2. When a steam helper engine pushed on the rear of the train, it would take 30 to 35 minutes after departing Lester before lumbering by Stampede. When that four-unit diesel helper was coupled on the head end of the three road units, Number 2 came flying by in *21 minutes!* Unbelievable.

Unbelievable, also—how brilliant the stars looked from high in the mountains, away from city lights.

I am most grateful for my opportunity to have worked at Stampede. It was a remarkable, unique time.

6506
6506
NORTHERN PACIFIC

PACIFIC

*Hooping up to Number 602 at Stampede, July 15, 1945.*

Stampede Day Operator Cody Caldwell has climbed up on a platform next to the track, called the pulpit, and is "hooping up" to engineer Frank Cavanaugh passing by in train Number 602. Cody had removed a staff from his machine and put it in a container on a round, metal hoop after using it to unlock the train order signal and setting it to the "proceed" position (see page 107 for diagram of a staff machine). Frank, the engineer, will throw this hoop off the train when passing the station at Martin, where the operator will reactivate the system by putting the staff in his machine. The canvas bag attached to the hoop provided three respirators—for the engineer, fireman, and head brakeman—in the event that the train should stall in the two-mile-long Stampede Tunnel. Respirators were rubber face masks containing a damp sponge.

The first time I hooped up to a train, I didn't let go quickly enough and just about pulled the fireman out of the cab. After getting the hang of it, an operator would drop the hoop on the engineman's arm with no tug at all.

The duties of the operators at Stampede and Martin were clearly defined and posted:

> Operators will wash and sterilize all respirators and sponges thrown off at their offices during their time on duty up to fifteen minutes before going off duty. Any respirators and sponges coming in during the last fifteen minutes of their shifts will be left for the next man.
>
> First trick operators will make time rolls, keep car reports, and make requisitions and any other clerical work required.
>
> Second trick operators will clean and fill all kerosene lamps including signal lamps.
>
> All operators will clean stoves, empty ashes, sweep floors, dust and fill all coal buckets before going off duty.

In the earlier 1940s, when I first worked at Martin and Stampede, the respirators were made of white rubber. Grimy fingerprints were extremely difficult to remove. We were supposed to clean them with an abrasive soap called Sapolio, but some operators would cheat and use kerosene, which was strictly forbidden because it was alleged to cause the rubber to deteriorate. As WWII progressed, rubber was in short supply, and a black substitute, much easier to clean, was used for the respirators. I almost felt guilty accepting the extra $17 per month we were paid for respirator care.

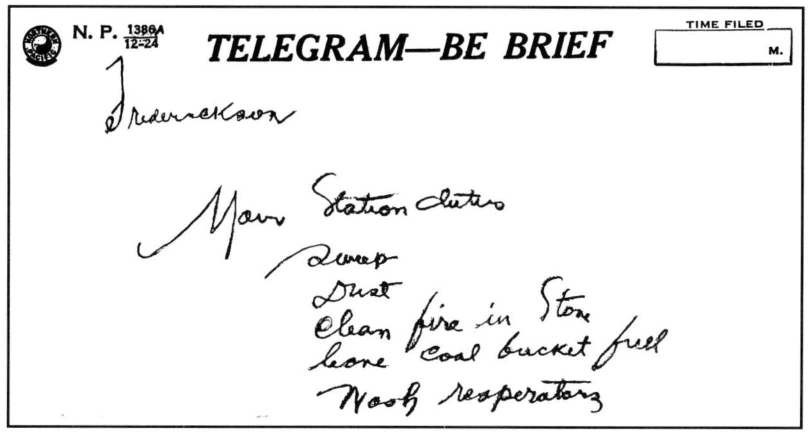
N. P. 1386A 12-24

TELEGRAM—BE BRIEF

TIME FILED ______ M.

Frederickson

Main Station duties

Sweep

Dust

Clean fire in Stove

leave coal bucket full

Wash resperators

*A copy of third-trick station duties at Stampede.*

*Cloud of soot and smoke from Tunnel 3 at Martin, summer 1944.*

"Trainmen Called it Stampede Hell" is the title of a story Max King wrote for the *Seattle Times,* describing the early days of Stampede Pass's nearly two-mile-long tunnel. There were no ventilating fans installed until over two decades after the tunnel was opened in 1888. Originally, it was hoped that prevailing winds from the west would clear smoke from the bore. However, since the tracks were an upgrade in both directions, and peaked near the center of the tunnel, it created a trap for engine smoke. Toxic gasses accumulated in the tunnel, especially if a strong wind wasn't blowing.

Max's story tells of a near tragic incident in 1912 when a long freight train stalled in the tunnel and several members of the crew were overcome by smoke, including the conductor, Bunyon Hezekiah Hamm. Fireman Jack Denise, however, remained conscious and, with the assistance of two section men, was able to drag the victims out of the tunnel to fresh air. The NP rewarded his heroism with a beautiful gold watch inscribed, "Presented to John S. Denise by the Northern Pacific Railway Company for bravery in rescuing men in the face of danger in the Stampede Tunnel, August 22, 1912." Denise later served as mayor of Auburn and became a U.S. Marshall in Western Washington.

The 1912 incident, in addition to some other close calls, hastened the installation of two giant fans at the tunnel's west portal to blow smoke out the east end. In 1915, when operation of the ventilating plant commenced, the fans were powered by a coal-fired steam engine. There always was fear that sparks from this engine might ignite the tunnel's wooden snow sheds. Finally in 1929, Puget Sound Power and Light brought electricity to Stampede and the fans were converted to electrical operation.

Vent plant operators were instructed to keep the fans blowing for twelve minutes after a train cleared the tunnel. Martin, on the east end of the tunnel, was enveloped by immense clouds of black, sooty smoke every time the fans were turned on. Any newcomer to Martin quickly learned not to hang laundry outside!

*BN rotary snowplow 42 with F-7 and GP-9 units at Lester, Washington, January 19, 1972.*

During my early years at Stampede Pass, the Northern Pacific stationed rotary snowplows at both Lester and Easton, on the ready for winter's fury. The end of the 1940s brought record-breaking snowfall and the rotaries often were used, along with their companion spreader trains. Since that time, snowfall has diminished somewhat, and diesel locomotives are better at shoving snow off the tracks than steam engines. When heavy snow does come, bulldozers and spreaders usually handle it adequately. Consequently, it is now a rarity to see a rotary snowplow at work.

When unusually heavy snows fell in January 1972, a rotary came to the rescue. Snowplows no longer were kept at Lester or Easton, but were stored in Seattle and Auburn. On January 19, a work train crew was called at Auburn to take Rotary 42 to the mountain, under the supervision of Trainmaster Jerry Bergman and Roadmaster Bob Robey, long-time friends of mine. They invited me to come along, provided I brought my camera. Of course, I jumped at the chance.

We went through the siding at Eagle Gorge to meet Amtrak Number 7. The next stop was Lester, where a final inspection was made of the plow and its pushers. After that, we spent the day plowing up the hill to Stampede and Martin and down the other side to Easton. Rotary 42 needed a regular diesel unit to provide power for its whirling blades. F-7 unit 9758 (formerly Spokane, Portland and Seattle 803) drew this assignment, and GP-9 unit 1921 (ex-NP 336) was the locomotive that pushed the plow train.

The responsibility usually fell to the roadmaster to keep the track open and to cope with whatever adversity mother nature brought. Max King, a long-time engineer over the mountain road, related that there was an old-time roadmaster who could look up at the top of Kelly Butte, high above Lester, and tell by the way the clouds were swirling if heavy snows were coming. There also is a legend about a rather inexperienced and arrogant roadmaster at Lester, who was called one stormy night by the section foreman at Martin and told it was snowing a foot an hour and that the rotary should be called. To which the roadmaster replied, "It can't snow that hard," and hung up—only to find out the next morning that Number 1 had stalled in the heavy snow.

Roadmaster Bob Robey used a scientific approach. He kept in touch with the government's Stampede Pass weather station on the Cascade crest above the railroad, which was exceptionally accurate in providing forecasts. Now and then Bob rewarded the men at the weather station with a gift designed to warm them up on cold winter nights.

N.P. 42
RADIO EQUIPPED
NORTHERN PACIFIC
NORTHERN PACIFIC RAILWAY
9758
SPOKANE PORTLAND SEATTLE

*Skiers boarding NP Number 5 at Martin, January 14, 1945.*

Before World War II, the most famous destination for skiers was the Union Pacific's Sun Valley, Idaho. It was an elaborate resort and widely publicized, notably by the Hollywood movie *Sun Valley Serenade* featuring the Glenn Miller orchestra. The Milwaukee Road had a popular skiing destination at Hyak on Snoqualmie Pass. Special "snow trains" ran on weekends to accommodate skiers who wanted to go to "An Ideal Winter Playground in the Heart of the Cascades." When Northern Pacific officials decided to promote skiing at Martin on Stampede Pass, the opposite ad appeared in Seattle newspapers.

Special train service wasn't provided, only the regular local trains—Number 4 going and Number 5 returning—with a little less than six hours between arrival and departure. The "especially equipped cars" were two old coaches outfitted with tables, located on the Tunnel Spur. Plans were made for a lodge; the first design was estimated at $100,000, which was considered impractical in light of the two-dollar ticket price. A scaled-down version was built on the north side of the tracks in 1941, but it was doomed by two strokes of bad luck—low snowfall and World War II. After the war, it was leased to the Associated Students of the University of Washington, who used it for a few years until it was destroyed by fire. In 1939, the Mountaineers, Inc., built a private lodge on the south side of the railroad called the Meany Ski Hut. It continues in use to this day.

I missed a good chance to become an entrepreneur during my wartime winters at Martin. Skiers still came to Martin on Number 4 even though the facilities weren't open. An hour or so before Number 5 was due they would knock on my door to ask if I had any refreshments for sale. I never did, but I should have—it would have been a wonderful opportunity to establish a fast food/beverage establishment with captive customer prices. I never did have much business sense.

## *NP Number 4, "The Alaskan," at Old Stampede, December 15, 1949.*

When my friend, NP Engineer Frank Scobee, saw this photo, he told me he really liked it and would appreciate a big enlargement. In the true tradition of Fredrickson's Fast Foto Service, it took me about 10 to 15 years to get it enlarged for him. It was only then that I found out why he wanted this particular picture.

The 2609 was Frank's favorite Class A engine, one of the original 4-8-4 Northern type. When completed in 1927, these engines were intended for exclusive use on the *North Coast Limited*. After being bumped off of this choice assignment by diesels, Class A's were used on freight trains as well as passenger service; some were on the Tacoma Division. On most of them the stroke on the valve gear had been lengthened for this dual service, but not on the 2609. Frank said, "you could hook her up so she would run like a sewing machine." He went on to reminisce about the time he had the 2609 on a troop train heading east and decided to see just what she could do. After passing Cle Elum, he pulled the throttle all the way back. Soon the fireman was hanging on with both hands and shouting, "My God, how fast are we going?!" Frank, having just timed the speed between mile posts, answered, "110 miles per hour."

I have an interesting addendum concerning the 2609. When steam engines were being scrapped at South Tacoma, the builders' plates were sold for a dollar. A builder's plate shows the name of the builder (Baldwin, Alco-Schenectady, etc.), the engine's serial number, and the year in which it was built. When I went out in 1954 to get one from a Class A engine, the only one available was from the 2609. I was disappointed, because I had hoped to get the plate of the 2600, the first of the Northerns, or from 2602, my particular favorite. Only since learning that I have the builder's plate from the locomotive that Frank Scobee ran at 110 mph have I realized that I possess a real treasure, and now it's one of the prizes in my collection.

*Builder's plate from the 2609.*

2609
2609
NORTHERN PACIFIC

*"North Coast Limited" at -30°, Easton, Washington, January 1950.*

Extremely cold weather encountered on the Northern Pacific's route usually occurs in Minnesota, North Dakota, or Montana, but Central Washington has experienced its frigid times, too. The winter of 1949–50 was "colder than the very darn dickens," as TV weatherman Ray Ramsey used to say. It was –30°F at Easton when I snapped this photo of the *North Coast Limited,* stopped for a diesel helper to be added to the head end. A few days earlier, I had taken a picture of a freight train stalled in the snow at Stampede during the still-remembered January 13 blizzard. Railroad workers possessed a special toughness to keep trains moving under such adversity and discomfort.

We experienced a minor cold-weather disaster in our living quarters in the rear of the New Stampede depot. My wife and I had gone to Tacoma during my two days off and when we returned, Cereta detrained at New Stampede while I went on through to Old Stampede to get our mail. The day operator at New Stampede, meaning to be helpful, had stoked a substantial fire in our coal stove to take the chill off our frigid quarters. Entering the kitchen, Cereta discovered that both the faucet and drain in the kitchen sink had been frozen, and the pipe behind the faucet had cracked. The warm fire had thawed the pipe and faucet, but not the drain, and water was running over onto the floor. Fortunately, she found some section men outside, who were able to drive a piece of wood into the crack and plug the leak. It meant another pipe-repair job for water serviceman Henry Gunther to add to his already long list of things to do. He had just about the most miserable job on the mountain, taking care of all the cold-weather plumbing problems in the company buildings.

6513
NORTHERN PACIFIC

*Neighborhood activity at Old Stampede, March 1950.*

The highlight of each day at a little place like Stampede was the arrival of the trains. Second trick telegrapher Denny Denzene, in the plaid jacket at the left, is waiting to get the mail. Because Lester was the nearest post office, where we all had mail boxes, Lester's agent-telegrapher collected our mail and sent it up on Number 4.

Anyone at Stampede who wanted to go shopping in town—Easton, Ellensburg, or Cle Elum—didn't have to worry about traffic or parking. We just boarded Number 4 headed east and came back on westbound Number 5 in the same afternoon. Shoppers could have three and a half hours in Cle Elum, a little less at Ellensburg, or a little more in Easton. This photo shows three of our neighbors waiting to board the train.

I was out with my camera this day to catch the first trip west of shiny, new engine 6513, which just had come out of the Electro-Motive factory in February. The little shed on the right housed Section Foreman Sam Campanelli's track car. The water tank remained for the rare appearance of a steam engine.

*Number 606 climbing Stampede Pass in the snow, December 2, 1967.*

Early one morning in the summer of 1985, before I was out of bed, the phone rang. The call was coming from two time zones east. I was thrilled to death after I bounced out of bed and listened to what the man on the other end was saying. It was David P. Morgan, the legendary Editor/Publisher of *Trains* magazine. He told me an upcoming issue would be featuring the Northern Pacific and he wanted to use one of my photos in the article. I have never filled a picture order faster! It was this photo of train Number 606 climbing Stampede Pass in the snow, which Morgan had seen in Charles R. Wood's *The Northern Pacific*.

I was even more thrilled when the article appeared in the December 1985 issue of *Trains*. There was my picture—a double-page spread leading off the article, with a title that brought joy to the hearts of all NP fans: "THE ALL-AMERICAN RAILROAD—We think this is the way to run a railroad." The first part reviewed other roads that were considered as "All-American" candidates and then the article said:

> So the nominee is Northern Pacific. It possessed the name, the heritage, the route, the trains, the scenery, the locomotives, the emblem to underwrite a consensus…Rich in heritage, following the trail of Lewis and Clark, created by an Act of Congress bearing the signature of A. Lincoln."

Four pages were devoted to reasons for his choice. There's one short paragraph I particularly liked:

> I never met a Northern Pacific man I didn't like, including the hogger who told me, "I wouldn't give one acre of Montana for the whole state of Wisconsin." [*Trains* is published in Milwaukee.]

Needless to say, this is one picture I am really glad I took. And it was on a fun trip. My son, Jim, was on the University of Puget Sound swim team in Tacoma, which was having a meet at Central Washington University in Ellensburg. Rather than drive across Snoqualmie Pass in a snowstorm, I elected to leave from Auburn on Number 606, which departed at 7:00 A.M. and would get me to Ellensburg in plenty of time for the meet. Engineer Ed Hurley was an old friend and we carried on a nostalgic conversation about our life on the railroad. After each anecdote—and there were many—Ed would say, "Those were the days my friend, we thought they'd never end." A cliché, I guess, but oh, so true.

GREAT NORTHERN
9724
BN
9724

*BN rotary snowplow waiting for the "Empire Builder" at Stampede, January 19, 1972.*

On a rotary snowplow ride I took in January 1972, we plowed the siding at Stampede and then waited for Amtrak's *Empire Builder* to go through the tunnel ahead of us.

It was somewhat sad that day to reflect on the past. In 1910 the Northern Pacific ran six passenger trains a day each way over Stampede Pass. When I went to work in 1943, three schedules each way remained. The *North Coast Limited* ran in two sections, one for Pullman sleeping-car passengers and the other for coach travelers, so there actually were four passenger trains each way. After the merger in 1970, Burlington Northern continued running two trains on this route, the *North Coast Limited* and the *Mainstreeter.*

On May 1, 1971, Amtrak took over operation of most of the nation's passenger trains and Stampede was down to one train each way. It was called the *Empire Builder,* taking the name of the Great Northern's premier train, thus ending the *North Coast Limited*'s reign as the nation's train operating the longest time under one name. Ten years later, Amtrak changed the route of the *Empire Builder* to Stevens Pass, so now only freight trains travel over Stampede, except for an occasional excursion special.

It's been rumored that both Burlington Northern Santa Fe and Amtrak would like to revert back to Stampede for the *Empire Builder,* but apparently the money to make the necessary changes isn't available. The State of Washington is studying the feasibility of establishing cross-state passenger service via Stampede and Yakima, with the possibility of some form of state financial assistance. It would be a great tourist attraction.

*Milwaukee "Olympian Hiawatha" detouring through Stampede Pass, 1949.*

If I somehow could be given a chance to retake one of my photos, this would be the one I would choose. The Milwaukee main line west of Easton was blocked by a slide or derailment and its Speedliner (as they called it), the *Olympian Hiawatha,* was detouring over the Northern Pacific from Easton, where there was an interchange track between the two railroads. The Milwaukee was electrified over the Cascades, but on the NP track, its train with a bi-polar electric motor had to be towed by an NP steam engine out of Easton. A helper engine also was needed for the climb over Stampede Pass so NP diesel 5410 was placed on the head end.

What a set-up for a great photo! Three types of locomotives—diesel, steam, and electric—and all together on one train! But luck wasn't with me that day. Unfortunately, the deep snow at Stampede made walking difficult. As the train approached, I was unable to get to a spot where all three engines could be seen together clearly through the lens of my old Graflex camera. I needed a wide-angle lens, but my camera had just the opposite. So, the diesel is okay, the steam engine shows somewhat, but the electric is just barely visible. What a shame to miss such an opportunity!

The passengers in the Skytop lounge car at the end of the Milwaukee's *Olympian Hiawatha* received an unexpected view of Stampede Pass on that sunny day because of the detour via the NP. At the left is the original Stampede station, which was converted to living quarters in 1914 when the New Stampede station was opened.

Ordinarily, *Olympian Hiawatha* passengers would be viewing Snoqualmie Pass, the Milwaukee route through the Cascades. The Great Northern's road was built over Stevens Pass. The three railroads had an agreement to allow the others to detour over their lines in case of a track obstruction. The connection at Easton between NP and Milwaukee made NP-Milwaukee detours the most common, although NP and GN could reroute through their subsidiary—the Spokane, Portland and Seattle—from Spokane or Pasco to Vancouver, Washington. On that fast track along the north bank of the Columbia River, the *North Coast Limited* or *Empire Builder* could reach Seattle reasonably close to on time.

The most out-of-the-way detour I remember occurred once when all three northern lines were blocked. NP's *North Coast Limited* to Seattle was rerouted via Union Pacific, running from Spokane to Portland along the south bank of the Columbia, and then back on NP track from Portland to Seattle.

Detours are a real pain in the neck for dispatchers. Fortunately, they were not a frequent occurrence.

BC-11
BC-11
NORTHERN ALBERTA
RAILWAYS

*Rail Travel Center/Mountain Outin'/Let's Travel Special at Dawson Creek, British Columbia, May 27, 1990.*

For a number of years I had the pleasure of being included on the staff of an annual special train tour on British Columbia Rail, chartered by Carl Fowler's Rail Travel Center, Rolland Graham's Mountain Outin' Tours, and Ed Von Nordeck's Let's Travel Tours. The tour's two-Budd cars traveled over almost all of the British Columbia Rail system, including the electrified Tumbler Ridge coal line and the freight-service-only lines from Prince George to Fort Nelson and from Chetwynd to Dawson Creek.

The 1990 visit to Dawson Creek had the added attraction of pulling into a historic Northern Alberta Railway station, rather than a British Columbia Rail freight stop. Dawson Creek, located in central British Columbia, was Milepost One on the Alaska Highway built during World War II. During the roadway's construction in 1942–43, special Northern Alberta Railway trains from Edmonton arrived there with American troops and workers. The station now is a museum, complete with a telegraph office occupied by a mannequin authentically dressed in a vest, bow tie, sleeve protectors, and a green eyeshade, the trademarks of a telegrapher.

After arriving at Dawson Creek, the tour entered the short and seldom-used connection to the Northern Alberta Railway, where the station was located. The track on this interchange was covered by tall grass, which obscured one important feature, a "derail." We went over it and it did what derails are supposed to do—it derailed us short of the station. A call was made to car men in Chetwynd to come and get us back on the track. Meanwhile, the passengers were loaded on buses to tour the town. I remained with the train to take pictures when it eventually pulled into the station. Patience paid off, but I suspected that this was the last time a train would arrive at Dawson Creek Station.

*Battleship "Missouri" and Puget Sound Naval Shipyard engine 11, Bremerton, Washington, October 16, 1974.*

When I was a child in Tacoma, the most exciting time of the year (in my opinion) was Fleet Week when ships of the U.S. Navy made an annual visit, usually around the Fourth of July. Destroyers and submarines tied up at the docks, and battleships and the larger cruisers anchored in Commencement Bay's deeper waters. Shore boats took visitors to the ships in the harbor from the Municipal Dock under the 11th Street Bridge.

I remember going aboard the battleships *Arizona*, *California*, *New Mexico*, and *Pennsylvania*, to mention a few (battleships were named for states). I also visited cruisers (which were named after cities), but no longer recall which ones. Battleships were my favorite, so it was thrilling to be invited to "go below" for a hot dog on one of them by a cousin serving as a cook; visitors usually were restricted to the main deck area.

During Fleet Week, the town swarmed with sailors. We kids couldn't get near the swings and slides at the Wright Park playground, as they were taken over by sailors and their girlfriends. At night, the ships aimed their powerful searchlights into the sky and rotated the beams for a spectacular display. The grand finale was the Fourth of July fireworks show at the Stadium Bowl. This was a breathtaking scene, with the sound of fireworks reverberating in the bowl, the close proximity of the rockets to the audience, and the warships standing at anchor in the bay. These gala festivities in Tacoma ceased in the early 1940s, however, as American involvement in World War II dispersed the fleet around the world.

In 1974, while in Bremerton on transportation assistant duties, I shot this photo of the mothballed battleship, U.S.S. *Missouri,* docked directly behind the Burlington Northern station on the waterfront. The *Missouri,* particularly significant as the ship on which the Japanese signed the documents of surrender in 1945, has since been sent to Pearl Harbor, Hawaii, as a permanent historic display—much to the disappointment of Bremerton.

63
P.S.N.S.
11
11
USN6500207

## *Northern Pacific wartime advertisement.*

The railroads were inundated after the United States entered World War II. Extra trains, with every available car, kept the rails humming. In addition, regular passenger service was filled to overflowing with military personnel being transferred and government workers sent on essential assignments. Railroad advertising completely reversed its message and requested nonessential travelers to not travel by rail. On the opposite page is a tactful example of such an ad, placed by the NP in 1942.

Another ad, published by the New York, New Haven and Hartford Railroad, became a classic. It was reprinted by the thousands and read on radio by the top celebrities of the time, among them Kate Smith, Eddie Cantor, and Ben Bernie.

That famous ad showed three young soldiers lying in their sleeping car berths, with the title:

> THE KID IN UPPER 4
>
> It is 3:42 on a troop train. Men wrapped in blankets are breathing heavily. Two in every lower berth. One in every upper. This is no ordinary trip. It may be their last in the U.S.A., till the end of the war. Tomorrow they will be on the high seas. One is wide awake... listening...staring into the blackness. *It is the kid in upper 4.*
>
> Tonight, he knows, he is leaving behind a lot of little things—and big ones. The taste of hamburgers and pop...the feel of driving a roadster over a six-lane highway...a dog named *Shucks, or Spot or Barnacle Bill*...The pretty girl who writes so often...that gray-haired man, so proud and awkward at the station...the mother who knit the socks he'll wear soon. Tonight he's thinking them over. There's a lump in his throat. And maybe—a tear fills his eyes. *It doesn't matter, Kid.* Nobody will see...it's too dark.
>
> A couple thousand miles away, where he's going they won't know him very well. But people all over the world are waiting, praying for him to come. *And he will come*, this kid in Upper 4. With new hope, peace and freedom for a tired, bleeding world.
>
> Next time you are on the train, *remember the kid in Upper 4.* If you have to stand en route–*it is so he may have a seat.* If there is no berth for you—*it is so he may sleep.* If you have to wait for a seat in the diner—it is so he...and thousands like him...*may have a meal they won't forget in the days to come.* For to treat him as our honored guest is the least we can do to pay a mighty debt of gratitude.

★ A Salute to the U. S. Navy — Navy Day, October 27 ★

# WE'RE in Action, too

**N**ORTHERN PACIFIC'S first responsibility today is war traffic and we're moving lots of it. Our fleet of freight and passenger cars and locomotives is in action, First to serve Uncle Sam and then to serve You.

Within War-time limitations, Northern Pacific continues to serve its patrons with the best possible accommodations whether you travel on business, "citizen furlough" or in the uniform of our armed forces.

The NORTH COAST LIMITED leaves daily for the Twin Cities and Chicago, via Yellowstone and the historic Lewis and Clark trail. Standard Pullmans, Tourist Cars and Coaches with "famously good" food at reasonable prices in the dining cars.

Make your reservations early. Avoid week-end departure, if possible. If your trip is postponed, please cancel Pullman space.

*For further information, write or call:*
1401 Fourth Avenue — ELiot 5560 — Seattle
N. J. HEUCHAN, *General Agent*

NORTHERN PACIFIC YELLOWSTONE PARK LINE

**NORTHERN PACIFIC RAILWAY**

*"Main Street of the Northwest"*

*Mrs. Floyd Crane stopping traffic in Tacoma for a Fort Lewis-bound troop train, 1944.*

During World War II, soldiers and sailors by the thousands were transported by train to various ports of embarkation on both coasts, where they boarded ships for overseas battlefronts. Fort Lewis, near Tacoma, was the origin or destination of countless troop trains. Finding enough equipment to accommodate the mass movement of so many men was a major problem. Every available coach, sleeper, dining car, and baggage car—no matter how ancient—was pressed into service. Troop sleeping cars and kitchen cars, which looked like box cars, were mass produced for troop train service.

The woman in this photo, Mrs. Floyd Crane, was one of many hired by the railroad to fill positions vacated by men who had joined the military. The dearth of qualified employees also made jobs available for teens too young for military service, as myself.

An additional assistant chief dispatcher position was created in Northern Pacific's Tacoma office to handle nothing but military moves. The brilliant Drayton "Zim" Zimmerman, who filled this position, was noted for his lengthy messages lining up the equipment and movement of troop trains. He and all those in the crucial dispatchers' office suffered intense mental stress during those trying times.

1766
DRINK
Coca-Cola
CRAN

## *Westbound troop train approaching Martin, Korean War era, 1952.*

There was constant fear of enemy sabotage during World War II. Guards were posted at tunnels, including old Tunnel 2 near where this photo was taken. On March 31, 1942, the Tacoma Division superintendent sent the following letter to all employees:

> All Concerned:
>
> We are all cautioned against any discussion of troop train movements on our line.
>
> These should not be mentioned to anyone, and this includes "best friends" and relatives. Claim is made by the Intelligence Department that:
>
> > A recent report is to the effect that this information leaks out through station agents, telegraph operators, and others, who, regardless of instructions that they may have received, tell friends when a troop train is due to arrive. These people spread the news, and it frequently happens that there is a large crowd at the station to meet the train. If the general public has the information, it is probable that enemy agents also have it, and are in a position to take such subversive action as they may consider feasible.
>
> The safe movement of troop trains is vital to the winning of the War, so don't hamper the War effort by loose talk.
>
> J.F. Alsip
> Superintendent

There was less fear of subversion during the Korean War, but civilians were not permitted to ride in troop train cars. The alternative for a deadheading employee was to ride in the engine. I was aboard the helper engine—a good place to be with a camera!

*Troop train bound for Fort Lewis, crossing Tacoma's Pacific Avenue, 1952.*

Moving of troops by train continued during the Korean Conflict (1950–53), but at a much smaller volume than in World War II. This train is made up of old heavyweight Pullman standard sleepers. The fifth car behind the engine is one of the troop kitchen cars built during the Second World War.

There have been continual changes in this scene over the years. The old Savoy and Croft Hotel, with the 7-UP sign, has been torn down. The double track line has been reduced to single track, as the result of a slipout a little farther up the line. Schoenfelds's Furniture no longer is in business, but the old structure has been restored to its original appearance and now is a medical building with Tully's Coffee on the street level. The new Tacoma Art Museum is being built on the right side of the track. The Tacoma Dome-to-downtown light rail line will cross the Burlington Northern and Santa Fe here. The site just behind where I took this photo is where the Northern Pacific "Villard" passenger station opened in 1884. This is the north gateway to the Union Station Historic District, which includes the Washington State History Museum and the University of Washington Tacoma Campus. Those of us who have spent a lifetime here are delighted with this progress in our city.

SCHOENFELDS
7up
HOTEL
Coca-Cola
1706
1706

*NP 44262, 40-foot boxcar at Half Moon Yard, Tacoma, September 15, 1969.*

In the April 1957 issue of *Tell Tale,* Northern Pacific's publication for employees, Robert Macfarlane said in his "Memo from the President" column:

> Incidentally, you may have noticed the 6-foot-high N.P.'s and the 8-foot Monads stenciled on the sides of box cars. With this more prominent identification, our box cars become more effective as "traveling bill boards" carrying our name and trademark into 48 states and Mexico.

The Northern Pacific trademark was attractive and, arguably, the most unique of all railroad logos, which induced NP to publish a booklet called *The Story of the Monad.* It tells how and why NP adopted this ancient symbol and the history and philosophy connected with it. To excerpt from the booklet:

> HOW AMERICA DISCOVERED THE MONAD
>
> At the Chicago World's Fair of 1893, E.H. McHenry, then Chief Engineer of the Northern Pacific, chanced to visit the Korean exhibit. Seeing the Korean flag, he was impressed by the simple but striking design it carried. Because at that time NP was searching for a suitable trademark, Mr. McHenry realized almost immediately that this symbol could be adapted quite readily for that purpose. When he returned to St. Paul he submitted his idea to Charles Fee, then General Passenger Agent, and together they worked out the emblem which today has become familiar to millions of Americans.

Regarding the meaning of the Monad, the booklet tells about the symbol's ancient origins in China and variations found in other countries, including North America where it has appeared in Pueblo Indian pottery and bead work of the Plains Indians. Then comes the philosophy:

> The primary force in the universe is a sort of impersonal "nature" rather than a personified deity or "god." These teachings hold that the Illimitable (probably "nature") produce the Great Extreme (the creative principle). From the Great Extreme came the Two Principles from which the rest of the world is descended.
>
> For the present explanation, which is of course greatly oversimplified, it is enough to say that these Two Principles are called the Yang and the Yin. Their primitive meanings were "Yang-Light; Yin-Darkness." Philosophically, they stood for the positive and negative. Further and later interpretations, and there are many, assigned them the meanings of force and matter, motion and rest, Heaven and Earth, male and female...
>
> The Monad's two comma shaped halves represent the Yang and the Yin.

There follows an explanation of Korean and Japanese variations and how the Monad is used by the Chinese as a charm to ward off evil influences.

The story concludes by saying:

> So it is, then, that in the Orient this ancient design has become the symbol of good luck. And in America—on Northern Pacific diesels, on passenger cars, freight cars, stationery, and traffic office windows—it has become the sign of good rail transportation. You'll see the Monad, too, on the side of new Northern Pacific Vista-Domes. Today, more than ever before, this age-old symbol stands for the newest, most modern passenger service...on one of the world's EXTRA-FINE trains... VISTA-DOME NORTH COAST LIMITED.

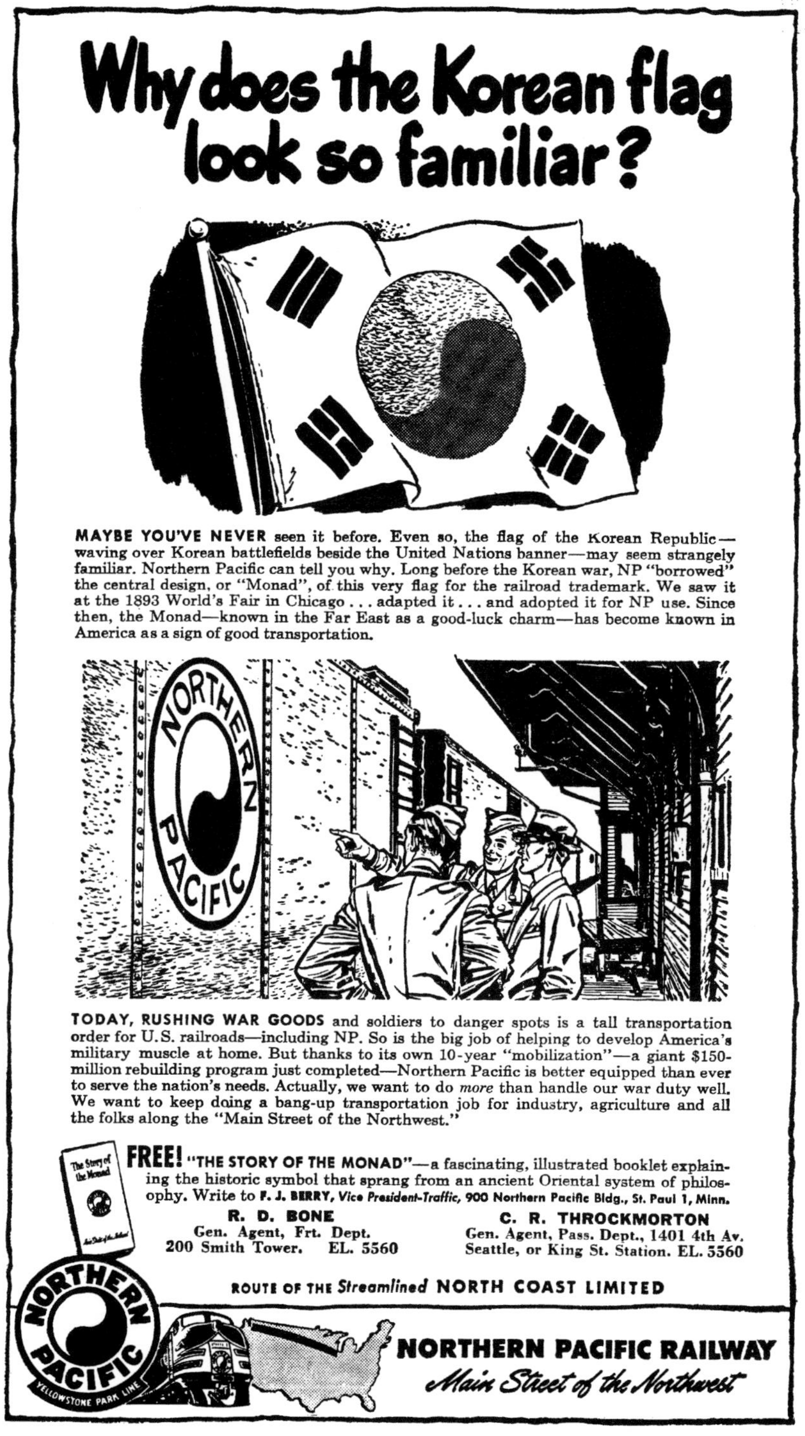


Seattle Times, *October 19, 1950.*

*Northern Pacific logo advertisement, April 1901.*

## *Throttle artists.*

George Fuhr became a Northern Pacific engineer on the Pacific Division on February 7, 1907. He ranked among the best. This photo of him illustrates the typical dress of a steam engineer, complete with overalls, gauntlet gloves, cap, and neckerchief to protect against cinders. The long-spouted oil can was used to lubricate bearings during station stops.

George was a mentor to my friend, Frank Scobee, who also became a noted throttle artist. Frank carried on the tradition of my heroes of the past on the mountain, such as Sivert Kvalheim, Bill Dahlberg, Ed Foisie, Jack Hodder, Louie Butt, and Jimmy Darker.

It was not uncommon on the NP— and probably most railroads—to find sons joining their fathers as "rails," although not necessarily in the same craft. Such was the case with the Scobees. Frank's father, Richard, began working for the NP as a signalman's helper at Paradise, Montana, on January 28, 1916, and became signal maintainer at Easton in 1923. I remember how friendly and helpful he was during my beginning days as a telegrapher there.

Francis William was one of five children born to Richard and Frances Scobee. After graduating from Easton High School in 1936, he immediately hired out on the NP, which had a roundhouse and facilities at Easton for the locomotives needed to help trains get over Stampede Pass.

He was employed as a caller, laborer, and engine watchman before becoming a fireman on September 3, 1940. Being a fireman was no easy job in the pre-diesel days. Most of the engines on the mountain were coal burners and some of them were hand-fired, which could mean up to 16 hours wielding the scoop. Another big event took place at that time for young Frank. He married Edlynn Miller, who had moved to Easton from Coos Bay, Oregon, to be a waitress in Ed's Cafe where most of the railroaders dined.

Bucking the extra board meant firing engines all over the division—to Sumas, Bellingham, Darrington, North Bend, and even on the south end to Portland. One day, Frank was given a tip by the clerk at the Seattle roundhouse that no one had bid on a vacant fireman's position on hot-shot Portland passenger train Number 408. Firemen with greater seniority than Frank had assumed that they didn't have a chance for this choice job, and didn't bid on it. Frank ended up the high bidder, and got to fire for one of the south end's throttle-masters, George Fuhr. George was the south end's answer to my ballast-scorching idols on the mountain.

Firing for these consummate professionals was a priceless experience for Frank and he was promoted to the right side of the cab on April 11, 1945, near the beginning of the ten-year transformation from steam to diesel power. The company became well aware of his exceptional skill at running a locomotive and he eventually was promoted to road foreman of engines in 1960 at Laurel, Montana. Later he moved on in that position to Livingston, Montana, then Missoula, and finally to Lewiston, Idaho. In 1968, he returned to his first love, handling an engine, and was engaged in passenger service between Seattle and Ellensburg, running the *North Coast Limited* and the *Mainstreeter*. When Amtrak took over passenger trains in 1971, Frank returned to freight service. He retired in 1978 after 42 years with NP.

In 1939, Frank and Edlynn had a son born in Cle Elum (12 miles east of Easton), whom they named Francis Richard Scobee to honor the previous two generations of Scobees. By the time he graduated from Auburn High School in 1957, "Dick," as he was nicknamed, had set his sights on flying. After starting as a flight mechanic, he learned to fly and became a combat pilot in Vietnam. His flying skills were as exceptional as the locomotive-handling talents of his father, and he was selected for astronaut training in 1978. Commander Francis R. Scobee piloted the Space Shuttle *Challenger* on a successful flight in 1984 and commanded it again when it was launched January 28, 1986. None of us who were present will ever forget the stunning tragedy when a blinding blast destroyed the *Challenger* and ended the lives of seven of America's finest. President Reagan spoke for us all when he said:

> We will never forget them, nor the last time we saw them, this morning, as they prepared for their journey and waved goodbye and slipped the surly bonds of earth to touch the face of God.

*South end throttle-master, Engineer George Fuhr, in Tacoma, May 11, 1944.*

*Engineer Frank Scobee, March 1972.*

## NP's first inspection car, 1915, from Wes Freeman's collection.

In 1915, a "contraption" was fabricated at the South Tacoma shops from the wrecks of three automobiles that had been on the losing end in encounters with trains. The engine was from a Hudson, the transmission off a Winton, and the chassis from a Stoddard-Dayton. The wooden-spoked wheels were designed by Shop Superintendent H.A. Lyddon and the car was put together by General Foreman John Metzger.

It was given the number 1915, for the year in which it was built. As NP's first bridge-inspection car, it was run as a train, carrying signals and markers, and with a conductor-pilot in charge. Although the 1915 was considered to be a five-passenger car, it often carried up to seven in an inspection party. Perhaps the tighter packing of individuals helped protect against the chill that earned the vehicle its nickname, "Pneumonia."

## The B-67, a superintendent's inspection car.

In later years, new automobiles were purchased for the division superintendents to serve as inspection cars. In 1939, most divisions were given Fords painted a bright yellow. These cars had rubber tires for highway travel and flanged wheels for the rails. The method for mounting or dismounting the tracks was ingenious. After a car was stopped, a turntable underneath it was dropped down and locked in place. Then the car could be elevated by means of a pump and prepared for the road or the rails.

In 1944, I photographed the B-67 at Easton when the boss stopped by for a visit. My friend Jerry Bergman was the secretary and driver for Tacoma Division superintendents I.P. Iverson and T.J. Kane. Years later, Jerry would have his own "hy-rail" vehicle—a big Suburban—when he himself became a division superintendent for BN at Lincoln, Nebraska, and Springfield, Illinois.

In 1943, I had a particularly memorable involvement regarding the superintendent's B-67. By the end of the year, I was feeling like I was a real part of the NP's Tacoma dispatchers' office and started publishing an in-house mimeographed newsletter, which I titled the *Monad*. (This was probably influenced by studying journalism at Stadium High School.) I featured a description of one of NP's locomotives and filled the rest of the page with division gossip.

Issue Number 1 came off without a hitch. Issue Number 2 was a different story. One of the dispatchers fed me two particular items for my gossip column that turned out to involve the superintendent and his B-67. The first read: "It has been rumored a certain farmer is trying to determine how his calf lost part of his tail and got his legs barked up. We wonder if this could be attributed to an Official's Tug-of War on a bridge a few weeks ago?" The second tidbit teased: "We would like to know more about the derailment that occurred at Everett on December 7th."

The first snide remark referred to an incident involving the occupants of the B-67 trying to extricate a calf that had gotten its legs caught between some ties on a bridge. The second comment related to a derailment of the B-67.

Issue Number 2 evidently proved to be too embarrassing for someone. Shortly after it was published, the word came down from on high: the *Monad* was suspended.

*Superintendent's inspection car at Eagle Gorge, December 1955.*

On August 7, 1955, at 3:00 P.M., Number 938, the Auburn to Cle Elum Local, Class W-3 steam engine 1763, with Conductor Harold Henricks and Engineer "Grandma" Wirachowsky, arrived at Eagle Gorge to find the station building engulfed in flames. It was a Sunday and the sole remaining telegrapher had returned to civilization for the weekend. (The second and third trick positions had been discontinued and the first trick had Saturday and Sunday off.) Telegraph service was temporarily suspended until September 12, when a new station housed in an old boxcar was opened.

In December of that year a massive slipout undermined the westward main track at Martin. Superintendent Worthington C. Smith, who had gone to the scene to supervise restoration of the main line, called me to come up with my camera and photograph the disaster. While there, I had a first-hand look at how lonely a position at the top can be. After the fill was restored, the moment came when the decision had to be made to resume train movements. The first candidate was Number 2, the *Mainstreeter*. It would be moving on the eastward track, perilously close to the newly restored westward. There was a multitude of roadmasters and engineering department personnel on hand and every last one of them said to Mr. Smith: "It's probably safe for Number 2, but it's up to you to decide." No one would give him absolute assurance that there would be no problems. He gave the word to let Number 2 proceed and collective breaths were held as it successfully crept by.

I returned to Tacoma with Mr. Smith in his hy-rail Jeep, the B-91. We stopped at Eagle Gorge for an update on trains in the territory. Eagle Gorge survived as a train order station until February 25, 1958, when it was closed permanently, leaving Kanaskat as the only open office between Auburn and Lester.

Construction of the Howard Hanson Dam made a line change to higher elevation necessary; this included the Eagle Gorge area. The little boxcar depot was moved to the new line, but never opened.

SANTA FE

## *Santa Fe train Number 12, "The Chicagoan," at Wichita, Kansas, July 20, 1940.*

At age 13, I had just begun taking pictures of trains. This photo of my father, Martin Fredrickson, standing near the Atchison, Topeka and Santa Fe *Chicagoan,* is the fourth in what has turned out to be a collection of thousands.

Each of the nation's railroads once operated its own fleet of regular and special passenger trains. The Santa Fe was as competitive as any when it came to innovative and unusual passenger service.

Probably the Santa Fe's most famous train was the *Death Valley Coyote Special*, one of the most remarkable passenger runs ever made. The following account of the *Coyote Special* is condensed from a Santa Fe commemorative brochure.

Just before noon on July 8, 1905, Mr. Walter Scott, a rich mine owner from Death Valley nicknamed "Death Valley Scotty," walked into the Los Angeles office of John Byrne, assistant passenger traffic manager for Santa Fe lines west of Albuquerque, and announced: "Mr. Byrne, I've been thinking of taking a train over your road to Chicago. I want you to put me there in forty-six hours. Kin you do it?"

Byrne whistled. "Forty-six hours? That's a lot faster than the eastbound run has ever been made. Do you realize that half the road is over mountain divisions?"

"I ought to," answered Scott. "I've been over the Santa Fe thirty-two times between here and Chicago. Here's the money!" And he began to shed $1,000 bills. "I'm willing to pay any figure, but I want to MAKE THE TIME! Kin you do it, or can't you! Let's talk business!"

The conference lasted a long time, and in the end Byrne put $5,500 in his safe. The train had been bought and paid for.

"Young man," said Mr. Byrne, "the Santa Fe will put you into Chicago in forty-six hours, if steam and steel hold together. We've got the roadbed, the equipment, and the men, don't forget that. But you'll be riding faster than a man ever rode before!"

"Pardner," said Scott simply, "I like your talk. Line 'em up all along the way and tell 'em we're coming."

Incredibly, all arrangements for what was to become known as the *Death Valley Coyote Special* were made within 24 hours. It pulled out of Santa Fe's La Grande Station in Los Angeles at 1:00 p.m., July 9, 1905, with a baggage car, a diner, and the Pullman car Muskegon. The Associated Press closely followed the *Coyote*'s progress, providing accounts to newspapers throughout the country, which gave the story preferred position on page one.

On the mountainous western half of the Santa Fe, the road's best engineers crowded the curves to the limit. Helper engines cut off on the fly at the summit of mountain grades, dashed ahead to the next siding, switched, and ducked in the clear an instant before the *Special* roared by. On descending grades, it was a matter of how fast the engineer dared run. Approaching Barstow, California, Engineer Finlay covered a mile in 39 seconds—96 mph! Nineteen different steam engines were used en route and changes were made in two minutes or less. Division superintendents were aboard across their territory. Huge crowds lined the track at stations.

The Santa Fe's "race track" commenced at La Junta, Colorado, with straight track on the level Kansas plains. "Scotty" rode the engine into Dodge City, describing passing telegraph poles as looking like a "fine-tooth comb." He wired President Theodore Roosevelt: "An American cowboy is coming East on a special train faster than any cowpuncher ever rode before; How much shall I break the transcontinental record?"

In Illinois, the streaking *Special* broke the speed record for a train, covering the 2.8 miles from Cameron to Surrey in one minute 35 seconds—106 mph. The previous record was 102 mph.

At 11:54 A.M., July 11, the famous train arrived at the Dearborn Street Station in Chicago; 2,265 miles had been covered in 44 hours and 54 minutes—13 hours and 2 minutes faster than the previous record.

Why did he do it? The Santa Fe explained:

> Persons who have a large surplus of ready money are privileged to indulge in fads and hobbies. One rich man collects rare paintings; another buys a yacht. John de Smyth spends a few millions for a big country estate; while Reginald van Rocks has a new auto every month. But until Walter Scott, no dollar-surfeited American ever chartered a special train to travel two-thirds of the way across the continent "just for the fun of it."

*Amtrak's "Southwest Chief," with Santa Fe locomotives, leaving Chicago, August 28, 1972.*

The Santa Fe line used to be synonymous with excellence in passenger train service. The Santa Fe operated many fine "name" trains, including the *Grand Canyon Limited,* the *El Capitan,* the *Missionary,* the *Navajo,* and the *Scout.* But three particularly were outstanding: the *California Limited,* the *Chief,* and the *Super Chief.*

Edward Ripley became president of the Santa Fe in 1896 and held this position for 24 years. He established the *California Limited,* running between Chicago and Los Angeles, which became the epitome of deluxe passenger train travel at the turn of the century, and the grandest and most popular train in the world. Each train was composed of 11 sleepers. In a peak season, there were as many as 45 *California Limited* trains operating on the system at a given time—22 eastbound and 23 westbound—a record never equalled.

In 1926, the year I was born, a new star streaked across the country on the Santa Fe rails: the *Chief.* It was advertised as the "New Santa Fe train deluxe, Extra fine, Extra fast, Extra fare."

In its advertisements, the Santa Fe lauded its new star:

> The *Chief* seems to have garnered much of California's compelling charm. As you step into its spacious cars complete in a perfection of readiness, you are at once captivated by that sensation of well-being, of all permeating comfort and enjoyment, which is the very essence of California.

The *California Limited* continued as a fast, sleeping-cars-only train, but dropped to the status of "second best."

In 1937 came a major breakthrough in passenger service with Santa Fe's inauguration of the *Super Chief,* the first diesel-powered, all-Pullman streamliner in the United States. Its Chicago–Los Angeles schedule was an incredible 34½ hours—14 hours faster than the steam-powered *Chief.* It was the first train to break the record of Death Valley Scotty's *Coyote Special* set in 1905. In accord with Santa Fe's reputation, the *Super Chief* also possessed the ultimate in luxury and fine dining. According to a Santa Fe advertisement:

> You're in the lap of luxury aboard the Super Chief. Gourmet Fred Harvey food. Impeccable service. Fun in the lavish lounges. Soft music. Superb scenery. VIP passenger list. If you want resort-stye luxury, travel Super Chief.

In the 1940s and '50s, the *Super Chief,* along with Union Pacific's *City of Los Angeles,* were the trains of the rich and famous. Those were the glory days of passenger train travel.

But the glory faded in the 1960s as air travel improved. When Amtrak took over U.S. passenger service in 1971, the super-luxury days had come to an end. At least Amtrak has kept alive a bit of the Santa Fe heritage with its *Southwest Chief* between Chicago and Los Angeles on the BNSF. One of the Santa Fe's services that Amtrak has retained is to provide Native American guides between Albuquerque and Gallup, New Mexico, to point out scenic highlights.

308
SANTA FE
SANTA FE

*First officers of the Monad Club, 1953.*

Of the million memories in my collection, none are more pleasant than those summoned by photos of the people and activities of the Monad Club, named after the NP trademark. Pictured here are the first officers of the club: (left to right) Elva Schrum, president; Charlotte Shaw, entertainment chairwoman; and Pearl Jacobson, secretary-treasurer.

Elva Pennant Schrum deserves sole credit for the idea of a service club to assist the Northern Pacific Hospital. For many years a crew caller, first at the Tacoma Roundhouse and later at the depot, Elva moved to Tacoma from England with her family, the Pennants, when she was ten years old. The Pennants were neighbors of Vince Lombardi, veteran machinist at the Tacoma Roundhouse. This led to NP careers for three of the Pennant children—brother Jack as a fireman starting in 1939; sister Madge Pennant Moak as a messenger at Tacoma Yard in 1944, then as a telegrapher and clerk; and Elva as a night caller at the roundhouse. Elva married switch tender Roy Schrum in 1947 and retired in 1971.

In January 1953, Elva decided something should be done to assist the NP hospital and she invited all of the women working at the depot to attend a meeting at her home to organize a club. Fund-raising was high on the agenda and periodic dances and bingo games at NP picnics added money to the treasury, which was used to buy the first television sets at the hospital and funded other improvements during the seventeen-year life of the club. The Monad Club was a symbol of the NP's spirit, but, like the trademark for which it was named, it faded away with the merger.

Charlotte Pappageorge Shaw went to work in the chief dispatcher's office in 1950, filling all of the caller and steno positions for most of a decade. In 1957 she married Asst. Claim Agent Jack Shaw, and in 1959 they were transferred to Glendive, Montana. This was the first of many moves as Jack climbed the ladder of success in his department. Eventually they were sent to St. Paul, where Jack served as Director of General Claims.

Pearl Jacobson was teaching school in Saskatchewan at a salary of $80 a month when she heard that the NP would pay 42 cents per hour to anyone who would enroll at the Spokane Telegraph School. At the completion of the six-month course, there was a promise of a job anywhere on the system, paying the astronomical salary of $200 a month. This was simply too good for Pearl to pass up. Upon graduating from telegraph school, Pearl chose the Tacoma Division, with 15th Street Tower in Tacoma as her first assignment. After working at Kelso and McCarver Street stations, she won a bid for a position at the Tacoma Union Station, and remained there until August 1, 1966, when she left to become treasurer-manager with the Western Division Northern Pacific Credit Union (known as WEDINOPA). Pearl had a reputation for phenomenal skill as a Morse telegrapher.

*Conductor Mickey Carr, Brakeman Lynn Smith, and Auditor Ernie Boyce on train Number 407, February 1956.*

One of the Northern Pacific's slogans, imprinted on all company pencils as a reminder, was "Courteous, Friendly." Those words were exemplified by this crew on Portland to Seattle train Number 407. They were in these positions because they liked people, and passenger service gave them an opportunity to meet and visit with the traveling public. On the flip side of the same token, freight service offered a refuge for those with more introverted personalities.

Train service assignments were awarded on the basis of seniority, so it generally took lots of "whiskers" to hold a passenger train position. For example, in this photo (left to right), Mickey Carr's date of employment was September 3, 1906; Lynn Smith's, June 1, 1914; and Ernie Boyce, the youngster of the group, started June 8, 1929. Together, they had a total of 119 years of service with the NP when I took this picture in 1956. Mickey's sleeve displays 10 five-year stars to commemorate his 50 years on the railroad.

## *NP Number 594 at Centralia, Washington, March 16, 1954.*

Saturday, March 16, 1954, marked the end of an era in Northern Pacific passenger service. That was the last day that the mixed train from Centralia ran to the Willapa Harbor communities of South Bend and Raymond.

Accommodations for passengers were provided in a combination coach-baggage car tacked on to the end of the daily (except Sunday) freight train. Freight service would continue, but the combination car would be discontinued.

At the division headquarters in Tacoma, Assistant Chief Dispatcher Don McGregor was in charge of allocating passenger cars. A few days before the last run of the mixed train, Don called Centralia Trainmaster Willard Thompson and volunteered to send a few extra coaches in the event a large crowd showed up to take the historic last ride.

Willard's response was, "Nah, don't bother, nobody cares about this slow old train to yesterday."

Don's apprehension was true to the mark. A large crowd did show up, many more than the old combination coach could carry. Two cabooses were hurriedly located in the freight yard and added behind the coach. All in all, it was a good move, as the many rail buffs were delighted to have a chance to ride in a caboose.

That's the surprised Willard carrying a suitcase, ready to board the train that so many people loved, but didn't patronize on a regular basis.

*NP dispatchers at Tacoma's Union Station, January 15, 1950.*

I was fortunate to have worked with extremely compatible associates. I can honestly say that there wasn't a train dispatcher in our Tacoma office who I didn't consider to be a close friend. Coming to work was a pleasure.

This photo was taken at what was known as "transfer time." A dispatcher of an incoming shift would show up about 15 minutes before going on duty to receive essential information from a dispatcher going off duty. Included in this picture are the fellows who will be taking over from three "trick" dispatchers and one assistant chief; the latter men have just finished the midnight to 8:00 A.M. third trick.

Standing, left to right, are: Dave Steinhoff, Dick Noble, Cam Galbreath, Reginald "RB" Lewis, Raymond "Smitty" Smith, Don McGregor, and Hal Bradbury. Jimmie Wyse is the seated man. Jimmie, Dave, and Hal were second generation railroaders, and all were seasoned veterans.

I dedicate this book to these dispatcher friends and all the rest in the Tacoma office who weren't present for this picture.

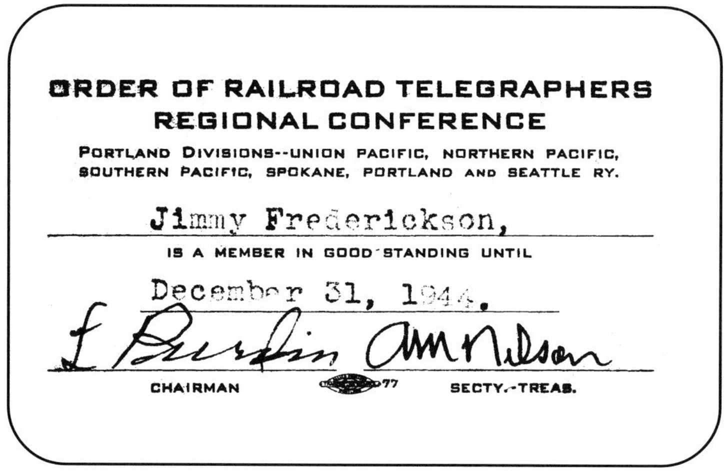
ORDER OF RAILROAD TELEGRAPHERS
REGIONAL CONFERENCE
PORTLAND DIVISIONS--UNION PACIFIC, NORTHERN PACIFIC, SOUTHERN PACIFIC, SPOKANE, PORTLAND AND SEATTLE RY.

Jimmy Frederickson,
IS A MEMBER IN GOOD STANDING UNTIL
December 31, 1944.

CHAIRMAN SECTY.-TREAS.

TIME TABLE

# INDEX